Overthinking:

How to Stop Overthinking, Escape Negative Thoughts, Declutter Your Mind, Relieve Stress & Anxiety, Build Mental Toughness & Live Fully

Thomas Swain

© Copyright 2021 - All rights reserved.

The content contained within this book may not be reproduced, duplicated or transmitted without direct written permission from the author or the publisher.

Under no circumstances will any blame or legal responsibility be held against the publisher, or author, for any damages, reparation, or monetary loss due to the information contained within this book, either directly or indirectly.

Legal Notice:
This book is copyright protected. It is only for personal use. You cannot amend, distribute, sell, use, quote or paraphrase any part, or the content within this book, without the consent of the author or publisher.

Disclaimer Notice:
Please note the information contained within this document is for educational and entertainment purposes only. All effort has been executed to present accurate, up to date, reliable, complete information. No warranties of any kind are declared or implied. Readers acknowledge that the author is not engaged in the rendering of legal, financial, medical or

professional advice. The content within this book has been derived from various sources. Please consult a licensed professional before attempting any techniques outlined in this book.

By reading this document, the reader agrees that under no circumstances is the author responsible for any losses, direct or indirect, that are incurred as a result of the use of the information contained within this document, including, but not limited to, errors, omissions, or inaccuracies.

Start Your Week The Right Way

We've all had that sinking feeling on a Sunday night, when you remember it's Monday tomorrow and the weekend is over. It can be tricky trying to launch ourselves back into work-mode, but with the right motivation and mentality, you can get your week off to the perfect start.

Receive evidence-based guidance, up-to-date resources, and first-hand accounts to help you.

Sign Up Now & You will receive this newsletter every Monday.

https://www.subscribepage.com/tswain

Contents

Introduction 1
Where does overthinking come from? 4
Stress 6
Anxiety 6
Depression 7
Decision making 7
Information Overload 8
Negativity Bias 10
Insomnia 10
Mental Health Conditions 11
Presenting solutions 11

Exploring The Reasons for Overthinking 14
Stress 14
Common causes of stress 16
The Two Types of Stress 17
Anxiety 20
Anxiety disorders 21
Depression and Rumination 23
Depression Symptoms 24

Causes of depression 25

Information Overload and Decision Making 26

Insomnia 28

Negativity Bias 29

Mental Health Conditions 30

Obsessive-Compulsive Disorder (OCD) 30

General Anxiety Disorder (GAD) 31

Cortisol 31

Escaping Overthinking 33

How to manage stress 33

How to manage anxiety 36

How to manage depression 41

How to manage information overload 45

Minimalism 50

How to make better decisions 53

How to manage Insomnia 55

How to manage medical conditions 57

Freedom From Negative Thoughts & The Negative Bias 58

Simple ways to deal with negative thoughts 61

Acceptance and Commitment Therapy (ACT) 61

Challenge your negative thoughts 64

Focus on your feelings right now 65

Socialize 66

Health and Fun 68

Distraction 69

Writing 70

Cognitive Restructuring 71

Cognitive Restructuring Steps 79

Positivity 85

Positive thinking begins with correct self-talk 87

Curate your own positive influences 90

Imagine your child once again 92

Gratitude 93

Self-Esteem 94

Causes of low self-esteem 96

How to have healthy self-esteem 97

Feel confident or fake it till you make it 98

Say no if you don't want to 99

Stop dwelling on any past regrets or negative experiences 99

Positive affirmations 100

Grow your strengths and work on your weaknesses 101

Be your own best friend 101

The Hierarchy of Needs 102

Level1: Physiological Needs 103

Level 2: Safety Needs 103

Level 3: Love and Belonging Needs 104

Level 4: Self-Esteem Needs 104

Level 5: Self-Actualization Needs 105

Meditation & Mindfulness 106

Meditation 106

Meditation and overthinking 108

Meditation and the brain 109

How to Meditate 113

Follow this step by step process to meditate 115

Walking meditation 117

Mindfulness 119

How to practice mindfulness 121

More Techniques, Tactics & Mindsets 125

Self awareness 126

Be kind 127

Questions 129

Think Big 131

Distraction 132

Philosophical razors 133

Occam's razor 134

Hanlon's razor 134

Change your stories 134

Exercise 136

Journaling 137

Set goals and stick to them 139

Mental Toughness 141

Can mental toughness be learned? 143

Let go of any self limiting beliefs 146

Break free from all or nothing thinking 146

Connect with your life purpose 148

Conclusion 150

References 161

Introduction

Thoughts travel faster than anything on planet earth. They are limitless in potential and can change in an instant. According to scientific data the brain can store around a million gigabytes and make more than a trillion connections through over one billion neurons. This equates to storing over three million hours of video or letting a movie run for over three hundred years in full high definition. Now that's just the storage capacity of the brain. Then there is the processing capacity of it. Human brains are far superior at processing than even the most advanced computers. Computers require millions of steps to calculate something which can be achieved using just a few hundred transmissions of brain neurons. Plus humans can make advanced plans, decisions and understand morality and humor.

Our superiority in cognitive ability and capacity sets us apart from the other animals on planet earth. However it is this same brain power that leaves us susceptible to overthinking. Taming such powerful brains to think clearly and calmly can be troublesome. Overthinking is a common issue. There are two forms of overthinking, worrying about the future or ruminating about the past. . Bad scenarios play out in their head like a hurricane of problems. Past troubles haunt them and the future burdens worry them. Even though most of these things never happened or it was never as bad as they imagined. Yet it still nags at them. Overthinkers tend to be very unrealistic and overly pessimistic. When things happen that they don't expect it can rock them and things can often get dark

"I can't stop thinking," or "I wish I had done this or I wish life was like that".

On and on it goes...

All of us can be affected by overthinking. We worry about our love life, our work life, our day to day responsibilities, the decisions we made in the past and so on. Essentially we are not in full control of our thoughts. Rather it is our thoughts that are controlling us. This can build up to unwanted negative results and a dimmer overall outlook on life. All of this of course has a ton of harmful side effects. Here are just a few of them.

- Difficulty to have normal conversations because you overthink how people will receive you.
- Constantly comparing yourself to others and feeling worse because you don't match up to them.
- Obsession over bad events that never happened.
- Stuck in the past, dwelling on your mistakes.
- Worrying about your future and doubting your abilities to succeed.
- Thoughts overwhelm you leading to worry, stress and anxiety.

Now is overthinking really a problem? I know what you're thinking (excuse the pun here). But I need to think? Thinking is a superpower of humans. Einstein thought about developing the theory of relativity. Newton thought about gravity. Elon Musk thinks about rockets and Justin Biebr thinks about music. Incidentally overthinking is ok. That's as long as you are aware of and in control of where your thoughts are going. The mind requires a solid foundation and establishing boundaries will help it to grow in the right direction. Those boundaries could come in limiting time to thinking, avoiding certain pathways such as negativity or focusing on a particular thing and nothing else.

Life becomes more enjoyable when you stop overthinking. When your mind is more free from the chains of overthinking it gives you the time and space to enjoy life. Without the mind numbing endless decisions you will inevitably make more positive things happen. Then you can spend time actually living life instead of just thinking about it or what might happen. Inner peace arises and your mind becomes free of worries, fears or regrets about the past or just mindless thoughts. Opportunities and joy will be abundant to you when you are more in the moment. All it takes is quieting the chatter of your mind. That can be done with ease.

Where does overthinking come from?

The human brain essentially is programmed to keep you alive and safe from prehistoric predators. Overthinking originates from the emotional part of your brain which is one of our primal preservation instincts. It is a speculative tool that will mostly analyze the worst possible perspective as a method of protecting you. Although it's not really beneficial in our modern world. For those of us who are more prone to overthinking this part of our brain is much more active. We tend to focus on the worst case scenarios because our brain is responding in a flight or fight mode. This mode exacerbates feelings of helplessness, stress and anxiety.

Imagine how it all plays out in the real world. Say you're working in a busy office and your boss asks you to try out a new reporting method. But you don't like it. So you explain why it's a bad idea to the boss. A debate spreads throughout the office. Suddenly you're to blame for the distraction and delay. But you didn't do anything wrong? You go home and think about what happened that day. In fact you think about it all night and it keeps you awake. Maybe your boss will fire you. Maybe your colleagues will hate you. Maybe it's time you find a new job. Maybe you should hand in your resignation notice tomorrow. At least you won't get fired. But maybe your boss is grateful for you highlighting this.

Going over this scenario is exhausting and most of these highly imagined scenarios will not even come true.

Each person has their own individual reasons for overthinking. Those depend on our own internal make up and our own life. That being said, there are some common themes to consider. In brief, here are some of the main reasons. We will explore them and their solutions in more detail later on.

Stress

When our mind is frantically seeking solutions it causes stress. The positive part of stress is that it is a result of real problems. That means those have real solutions. Therefore eventually those problems can be resolved and in turn escape the hold of overthinking. The difference between anxiety and stress is that anxiety does not have any logical or real world causes.

Anxiety

Anxiety is a leading cause of overthinking. The NHS recently reported that one in five adults in the UK suffer from generalised anxiety disorder (GAD). Often it begins with logic but this often spirals into much less logical directions. Like a fire burning hotter the more you think about it the more it grows. Anxiety and overthinking are very closely linked. We fail to live in the present moment but get anxious about the past or future worries.

Depression

Excessive overthinking creates feelings of distress that can lead to depression. This also goes the other way. A depressed person often is overthinking how bad things are. They ruminate and the thoughts cycle around their minds. It can lead to regret, self-loathing and blame. Rumination is usually a catalyst of developing depression.

Decision making

Many of us struggle when it comes to making decisions. We feel it's normal to think in detail about decisions. But at what point does it become irrational to overthink decisions? Well that all depends on the context. Everyday we are presented with decisions. From what food to eat to bigger decisions such as who to marry or what company to work for and so on. Indeed some decisions do require more thought. But it should be a deliberate and active way of thinking. Thinking that we might make a wrong choice can be paralyzing. It is a difficult road to navigate. Most people get stuck here because they fear failure or being wrong. Overthinking small decisions will lead us astray. Instead of taking action and sticking with a decision the overthinker breaks it apart and down into an intellectual debate. Something simple ends up becoming quite complex. The failure of overthinking is that it prevents real thinking from taking place. Instead there is a swarm of ideas and scenarios going around without any real meaning.

Information Overload

Our modern high-tech world everyday overwhelms us with new stimuli. But it is also an exciting one that should be lived with joy. Music, television, social media and so many other sources offer us an abundance of information that is accessible at any time. Never before have we been able to curate our world like this. Think about it, in the not too distant past we had to watch whatever show was on at that particular time. Back then there were limited choices as to how we spent our time and as such there was much less to think about. Nowadays we have so many choices that simple decisions such as deciding what to eat can create brain overload. Stuck in thought we are left unable to live fully.

Such an energetic and abundant world can be an overwhelming place. The overthinking person feels, sees and hears everything much more. Fine details of life overfill their minds and memories. Thoughts are broken down to the smallest of details. Too much is going on. Too much to process and too much inevitably leads to burnout, anxiety and stress. Life becomes difficult to process and the results end up even more overwhelming. This is the trap of overthinking and it goes on like water swirling down a sinkhole, speeding up and out of control.

"It's not a daily increase, but a daily decrease. Hack away at the inessentials."

– Bruce Lee

Negativity Bias

For millions of years the human nervous system evolved to what it is today. But it has remained the same as when we were at the risk of being faced with man-eating predators. That same response to keep us safe and alive tends to overestimate threats and underestimate opportunities. This is known as the negativity bias and is essentially our human default to react more intensely to the neafbe than the positive. In terms of thinking it causes us to overthink and worry more than is necessary. We are no longer a primitive cave species. The modern world is a far safer place.

Insomnia

Picture the scene. You're in bed ready to sleep but you're still wide awake. You think, "I have just eight hours to sleep before work." So you check your phone, scroll through some notifications and one more hour has passed. But you still haven't slept a wink. Thoughts start to crowd your mind. Round and round the thoughts go. This makes you obsessed which makes you more tired but unable to sleep because your mind just won't switch off.

Mental Health Conditions

As you can see there are a multitude of reasons for overthinking. Each individual has their own triggers and reasons. Then there are some which are the result of medical and health conditions. Those include Obsessive-Compulsive Disorder (OCD) or General Anxiety Disorder (GAD). More serious long term depression can also be a type of mental illness that causes over thinking. If you suffer from such conditions please seek medical advice or contact a mental health professional.

Presenting solutions

Realize that you are in control of your own thoughts and actions. Indeed sometimes a little bit of worry about the future or reflection on the past is healthy. That can help us become better. The difference between that and overthinking is that the latter is more passive than active. Awareness of your overthinking is the first step to making a change. When you recognize that it does you more harm than good then you're on your way to a positive evolution. Indeed we can change outcomes of future events happening. But we can't imagine that into reality. Instead of thinking about it, we actually need to take action. Ready, aim fire. It's all a quick sequence. Remind yourself that you cannot control other people. You cannot change what they think or do. They are the ones in control of themselves.

Don't despair and think there is nothing you can do from here. This book was written specifically to solve your overthinking. In fact there are several exercises and mindsets that will help you to escape overthinking. First we will take a look at the causes. Then we will look at some of the ways you can upgrade your thinking. From self-esteem to mindfulness, mental toughness and much more. In the conclusion we will explore the promises made and summarize the key points.

My name is Thomas Swain. Like millions of others I struggled and failed in search of success and happiness. Growing up I had a blurred vision of my goals in life. I thought money, fame and success would be the answer. Yet I was unsatisfied. I struggled with insomnia and stress. Through the ups and downs I found peace of mind in the concepts outlined in this book. A common struggle of many people right now. I promise you overthinking can be healed. In this book allow me to outline some of the ways and we will work on it together. With consistency in your practice your mind will become calmer and less likely to spiral out of control.

Let us make sure our thinking is useful to us. When thinking, let's aim for clarity and control. Recognize when we get stuck in anxiety and confusion. Seek help from others and be forgiving of yourself. Don't avoid the pain points. Look at the negatives and how you can work on making them positives.

Now let us harness our super brain power!

Exploring The Reasons for Overthinking

Every person has their own individual reasons for overthinking. Those depend on our genetic make up, our own life circumstances and the events that shape us. That being said, there are some common reasons to consider. Let's take a look and explore them in this chapter. In the next chapter we will explore solutions to them. But first to be effective and break free from overthinking we need to understand the reasons behind it.

Stress

Stress is a part of everyday life. It is how our body responds to pressure by releasing the stress hormones of cortisol and adrenaline. Life events can trigger us to feel more or less of this pressure. Unfortunately there is not really a universal medical definition of what stress is. Because of this, health care professionals often disagree as to whether or not stress causes certain problems or is the result of them. Naturally this makes it difficult to identify stress and resolve it.

Truth is that we all feel stressed sometimes. It can even motivate or help us. For the success driven person it can often become a way of life. Our ability to cope is unique to each of us. It depends on our genetics, life experience and circumstances. But for other people, the things we can cope with might overwhelm them. In the worst case it can negatively affect a person's life resulting in many unwanted effects both physically and mentally.

When you're constantly stressed out it can become a serious health issue. Identifying the causes of your stress makes it easier to manage. Consider some of the most common causes of stress. Do any of these sound familiar to you?

Common causes of stress

- Stress at work – maybe you're under pressure at work. Or you have recently become unemployed or retired.
- Family stress – maybe you're experiencing relationship problems at the moment. You might be going through a breakup or having an affair.
- Financial stress – suddenly you have huge bills to pay and you need to borrow money. There's just not enough money for the month and so on.
- Health problems – maybe you were recently diagnosed with an illness, suffered an injury or lost someone you love.
- Stress from life in general - various life events from buying a dress for a wedding to planning for a holiday can all lead to feelings of stress.

Physical symptoms of stress include

- Headaches and or dizziness
- Muscle pain and or tension
- Stomach issues
- Chest pains and or a faster heartbeat
- Sexual issues

Mental symptoms of stress include

- Find it difficult to concentrate
- Find it difficult to make decisions
- Often overwhelmed
- Worrying too much
- Forgetful

How stress can cause changes in behaviour

- Irritable and moody
- Not enough or too much sleep
- Not eating enough or eating too much
- Avoidance of people or certain places
- Drinking, drugs or smoking

The Two Types of Stress

The National Institute of Mental Health (NIMH) recognizes that there are two types of stress. Those are, acute stress and chronic stress.

Acute stress

Acute stress is the most common type of stress. People who are faced with pressure from recent events or upcoming challenges in the near future are likely to experience this type of stress.

For example maybe you were stressed out about a recent disagreement or you have an upcoming deadline. Since the solutions tend to be clear and immediate acute stress is usually easier to overcome. Even with the most difficult of challenges there is often a clear way out.

Fortunately because acute stress is short term it does not create any long term side effects. Usually you will be faced with short term side effects such as headaches, muscle tension, stomach ache or general distress. However if acute stress is repetitive it can become a long standing problem and you should seek professional medical advice.

Chronic stress

Chronic stress develops over longer time periods and can be much more harmful to us. Causes are usually life circumstances such as a dysfunctional family, relationship problems, ongoing poverty or various other stresses. Additionally, early life traumatic experiences can also cause chronic stress. Chronic stress can contribute to cardiovascular, immune, sleep, respiratory and reproductive problems.

Overthinking

When a person is in a constant state of chronic stress it can lead to serious health problems such as diabetes, high blood pressure and heart problems. Mentally it can cause depression, post-traumatic stress disorder (PTSD), and many more real issues. If it continues unnoticed people are left feeling hopeless. Inevitably this could lead to a breakdown which may result in violence or even suicide. Again if you suffer from any of these issues please seek professional help.

The NIMH have concluded that there are three clear causes of stress:

Routine stress

This occurs from daily activities such as taking care of children, homework or finances and so on.

Sudden, disruptive changes

This occurs when there is a sudden change from normal life. That could be something like a job loss or a family bereavement.

Traumatic stress

This occurs as a result of extreme trauma such as an accident, assault, war, disaster and so on.

Anxiety

Anxiety is a normal emotion. According to The American Psychological Association (APA) it is;

"An emotion characterized by feelings of tension, worried thoughts and physical changes like increased blood pressure."

We all experience anxiety on some level. It only becomes a problem when people experience excessive levels of anxiety. On a mild level it can cause some unsettling feelings. Whilst at more severe levels it can greatly affect daily life leading to excessive fears, worry and nervousness. Worst case scenario it could develop into a health problem or a serious medical disorder. Such disorders affect behaviour and emotions. Understanding the differences between normal anxiety and General Anxiety Disorder (GAD) which requires medical attention can help people to overcome their conditions.

Overthinking

When faced with potentially harmful or worrying situations it is normal for humans to feel anxious. In fact it is necessary for survival. Since the beginning of human evolution predators have approached humans and set off alarms in their biology. Dangerous situations create an adrenaline rush of hormones from the brains which triggers anxiety. These cause noticeable effects such as a faster heartbeat, sweating and alertness. This is otherwise known as the "fight-or-flight' response and it serves to protect humans from potential threats.

Of course nowadays that isn't much use because we are no longer being chased by large predators. However events in daily life still create this response. This is usually an overreaction that sends us into anxiety. Sure in some situations such as dangerous ones it is a vital signal. But it is mostly unnecessary and not serving our benefit. Rather it is clouding our judgement and hurting our life.

Anxiety disorders

In extreme cases anxious feelings are out of proportion to the trigger cause or event. This is when anxiety goes further into becoming

General Anxiety Disorder (GAD). Over reactions can cause physical symptoms including high blood pressure and nausea. The APA describes GAD as;

"having recurring intrusive thoughts or concerns." When anxiety becomes a disorder it begins to negatively impact daily life.

Nearly forty million people are affected by GAD in the United States alone. In fact it is one of the most common mental illnesses. Unfortunately GAD doesn't have any instant solution. However it can be effectively managed and less problematic through the use of specific tools and therapy. Symptoms of GAD include.

- Constant restlessness
- Unable to control feelings of worry
- Easily irritabile
- Find it difficult to concentrate
- Problems with slee
- Sleep difficulties
- Disruption of daily life

Depression and Rumination

Almost ten percent of the U.S adult population have at least one time experienced a significant bout of depression within the last year. People from all ages, races, ethnicities and socioeconomic backgrounds can experience depression. Some are lucky and will maybe only experience one depressive experience during their lifetime. But for many it can last much longer. Beyond feeling sad or going through a rough patch, those with depressive disorders have a serious mental health condition. Without treatment it can wreak havoc on their lives. Fortunately with professional medication and treatment they can become better.

Overthinkers are often left feeling depressed. It can feel like a never ending cycle of negative thoughts. This can cause lower energy levels and make them withdraw from social life. Simple daily activities can become overwhelming. On a biological level depression takes over the prefrontal cortex which is the logical thinking part of our brain. As a result of this hijack the brain is left feeling negative and hopeless. Indeed we all have negative thoughts now and then. It's completely normal to feel sad or down sometimes. That's just how life can go.

The problem is that these negative thoughts can start to continually replay in our minds. This is known as rumination and it is a danger to our mental health. The more it prolongs the more it can intensify depression and our ability to think clearly.

Depression Symptoms

There are a number of different symptoms of depression which depend on the individual. Usually it changes each day and a depressive episode lasts upto two weeks for the average person. Some common symptoms include.

- Insomnia
- Difficulty to concentrate
- Lower energy and less activity
- Lacking interest in activities
- Feelings of hopelessness
- Sleep inconsistency
- Appetite inconsistency
- Low interest in activities
- Hopelessness, suicidal or guilty thoughts

Causes of depression

There is no one single cause for depression. It can come about because of a number of reasons. Anything from a life crisis, physical illness or other stresses that occur in your life can contribute to depressive episodes. Consider some of these other common causes of depression.

Trauma

Some other causes of depression to take into account are traumas. People who have experienced a trauma when they were younger can be left with changes in their brains which might lead to depression. The same can be said for genetics. Some disorders tend to run in the family.

Life circumstances

Changes in life circumstances can influence a person developing depression. Some of those might be romantic status, changes in career, financial issues and general life changes. Or even where a person lives or works.

Medical conditions

People who have chronic illnesses and ongoing pains are more likely to experience depression. Some medications may also cause depression as a side effect. Consider what you put into your body.

Drug and alcohol misuse

Nearly a quarter of adults with substance abuse issues are reported to have experienced major depressive episodes. Usually they are abusing drugs or alcohol to escape their depression and overthinking. But it's a trap of cycling into something much worse. Treatment for both problems is the solution. Again consider what you put into your body.

Information Overload and Decision Making

Consider all of the information that comes your way on a daily basis. In today's modern digital world there is an avalanche of information coming at us every moment. Too much of it will overwhelm you. Add to this that when you have been living in the same place for a while it's natural to accumulate a lot of stuff. The same holds true in the digital domain. We store an excess of stuff that clogs up our laptops, phones and devices. Most of this stuff is unnecessary and it clouds our thinking. We are filling our lives with stuff that we really don't need. All of that fills up space in your mind too. Mental freedom is compromised and it sucks your productivity and clouds your thinking.

For many of us this is a paradox. On one hand it is great having all of this choice. Whilst on the other hand it is disrupting our lives. It causes us to procrastinate simple decisions and be overwhelmed with all of the choices. The present world we are living in right now is a place of abundance. Masters of our realms we can curate the finest details of our lives. From what we eat to what we watch on the TV. Just imagine fifty years ago. You had to watch what was on TV at that moment. Whilst choices of what to eat or who to date were much more limited. Clearly we are in a much better place nowadays. However research has shown that having more choices can increase anxiety, paralysis and dissatisfaction. This is known as the paradox of choice. The author Barry Schwartz, observed that having more options to choose from doesn't necessarily make people more happy but it can cause them stress and make decisions difficult. Try focusing on an excess of life experience instead and live with a minimalist attitude towards materialism. More on this later in the chapter.

Insomnia

Picture this familiar scene. It's already past bedtime.You're in bed ready to sleep but you're still wide awake. Your mind races and thinks, "I have just eight hours to sleep before work". You check your phone and one hour has passed. The phone light fills the room. Still you haven't slept a wink. Thoughts start to crowd your mind. Round and round the thoughts go and make you more tired but unable to sleep because your mind just won't switch off. The mistake many of us might make in this situation is to medicate. As you will find out later on, in most cases it is better to ride the dragon in a natural way than to lock it in a cupboard using medicine. We will explore natural remedies with far superior long term benefits.

Negativity Bias

For over six hundred million years the human nervous system has been evolving. Yet it is still responding in the same ways to life threatening survival situations. In order to keep us safe and alive the human brain evolved to overestimate threats whilst underestimating opportunities and resources. This is known as the negativity bias which essentially is the human tendency to react more intensely to negative stimulus than positive.

When it comes to our thinking this translates to a default of overthinking and worrying more than is necessary. Threats and challenges are seen as much more than they really are. But we are no longer a primitive species living in caves. The modern world is a relatively much safer place.

The more we perceive something to be out of our control the more it can worry us. We try to think up every way to gain control. This is a difficult pattern to escape from. Many people don't want to have to suffer the shame of being a failure. So they get stuck thinking of how not to fail. Catastrophes are imagined. The worst case scenarios are thought up in detail.

Inevitably the thoughts spiral faster and faster out of control.

Mental Health Conditions

There are numerous reasons for overthinking. Of course these differ for each individual. As we explored many come from life situations and damaged thinking. Then there are some which are caused by health conditions. Mainly those include Obsessive-Compulsive Disorder (OCD) and General Anxiety Disorder (GAD). Depression is another mental illness that causes negative thinking. See the earlier section for more information on that. Also I will present solutions to that later on.

Obsessive-Compulsive Disorder (OCD)

OCD is a condition where a person experiences recurring thoughts or frequent behaviours that they cannot control. If you experience symptoms whereby you're having unpleasant thoughts or negative behaviours then consider talking with a therapist. Additionally there are some medicines that may help with more severe symptoms of OCD.

General Anxiety Disorder (GAD)

GAD is a condition where a person feels anxious most of the time. If you experience symptoms such as constant worry, a sense of dread or trouble concentrating then you may require treatment or medicine.

Cortisol

Additionally when we are under stress the body releases the hormone called Cortisol. The right balance of this hormone is essential for our health. However when we are under too much stress it makes our brain think we are in danger and so our cortisol levels become dangerously high. As a result the body becomes weary and tired. At worst it can cause heart attacks, anxiety, depression and mental illness.

Again, If you suffer from any of these conditions please contact a mental health professional for medical advice.

Now we have explored the causes of overthinking. This was an important step to take. As I mentioned, to effectively break free from overthinking you first need to understand the causes. Now with that in mind in the next chapter specific solutions to those causes will be presented.

Escaping Overthinking

In the previous chapter we looked at the main reasons for overthinking. Getting to the root of a problem is the best way to treat it. Now we can begin to come up with specific solutions to those specific causes. Let's explore.

How to manage stress

Managing stress effectively begins with recognizing when it is a problem. As I mentioned earlier some people use stress to fuel them. Think of that high powered executive burning off the fuels of stress to get through his hectic work day. That's not a great lifestyle. Eventually he will burn out or end up in a hospital. Plus there is an alternative where you could be achieving much better results with much more fulfillment. Remember you're not a superhero.

So what's the solution? First of all identify if you're experiencing any of the physical warning signs of stress. Do you suffer from tense muscles, headaches or tiredness? Identify any mental or behavioural warning signs of stress.

- Do you find it difficult to concentrate or make decisions?
- Are you often overwhelmed, forgetful or tend to worry too much?
- Do you find yourself to often be moody?
- Are you getting enough sleep or having too much?
- Are you eating right?
- Are you avoiding anyone or anything?

If you have identified any warning signs of stress, start to think about what is causing the stress. It could be coming from any of the areas I mentioned earlier.

Summary of common causes of stress

- Stress at work
- Family stress
- Financial stress
- Health problems
- Stress from life in general

Sort any issue into lists with practical solutions. Now that you have possible solutions out in front of you it's time to take small steps towards change. Make a plan to address whatever you can. Simple solutions could be cutting down on commitments, saying no or trying a new life change. Whatever it is, stick with it.

Review your lifestyle. You could well be taking on way too much. In that case it might be a good idea to delegate. Or you could just prioritize your life and focus more on what's important to you. Focus on cultivating supportive relationships. Spend time to cultivate and grow the relationships that really matter. Spend quality time with your friends and family. If you're lonely then expand your social life. Join some clubs, hobbies and activities. All these will have a positive impact on your life.

Finally build positive and healthy life habits. Make sure you are eating healthy. Plenty of nutrients and clean food. Workout consistently. Mix it up with cardio and weights. If you hate working out, join a sports club or a fitness class. There are so many ways to get fit. No excuses. If you smoke, drink or take drugs try to cut it out or stop it entirely. Give yourself some nice well earned breaks now and then. Go for a walk in nature. Or when you get really burned out take a nice long beach holiday. Get some quality sleep in by having a consistent bedtime and a consistent wake up time.

If you still struggle with stress then consider getting professional help. That doesn't mean you're a failure. Your health is paramount and professionals can give you a lift up. With their expertise they will be able to advise and treat you further.

How to manage anxiety

A life with anxiety can be troublesome. However don't worry because there are clear steps that can help you to manage it. First of all realize that anxiety has less strength when you focus your attention to the present moment. Clear your mind. When your anxiety levels rise, start to get back control by taking some deep breaths. This can restore harmony and center you back into the present moment. Try this simple exercise out. Follow the steps below.
- Sit in a comfortable position. Or lean against a wall.

- Close your eyes. Now begin to slowly breathe in through your nostrils. Follow this with a long breath out through your mouth.
- Try using a mantra as you are breathing in and out. It could be "present". Or "now". Whatever you prefer. Say it out loud as you breathe out.
- Keep practicing this powerful breathing exercise to make you stronger at fighting anxiety and staying present.

*For a more detailed version of this you can check out the meditation and mindfulness chapter.

Get to the root of your problem

Anxiety presents physical symptoms which can be overwhelming. Your heart beats out of control, you tremble and feel pain. Overwhelming, a big distraction that catches up your attention and cycles into a worse situation.

Discovering a solution requires getting to the root of what is causing the anxiety. Make some time to explore your feelings and thoughts. Using a journal to write your feelings can be a powerful tool for exploring the causes of your anxiety. Keep it beside your bed or in your work bag so that you can have easy access to it. Cultivate the habit of exploring the causes of your anxiety. In time you will work on solutions to the root cause. Yes, that will be much more powerful than dealing with the symptoms.

Each of us has our own triggers for anxiety. They can sometimes be obvious things such as too much caffeine, alcohol or smoking. Then sometimes it could be less obvious. Maybe it comes from financial or relationship situations. However if you can identify the trigger then you can limit your exposure and response to it. Below are some of the most common triggers.

- Work related stress
- Relationships
- Genetics
- Withdrawal from medication or drugs
- Side effects of medication or drugs
- Driving or traveling
- Trauma
- Phobias such as fear of crowds or heights
- Chronic illnesses or pain
- Caffeine

Focus on solutions

Anxiety is often the result of fears from events that have never happened or are unlikely to happen. As an example we worry that our job will be lost or that we might become ill. Indeed life presents us with surprises and bad things often happen. You can't control that. Instead of focusing on what you can't control, focus on solutions. A powerful solution is to let go of that fear and focus on what you're grateful for. When bad things do actually happen instead of being imagined you also have the choice of how you respond to them. This is bringing the power back to you and away from the grip of anxiety. With practice you will effectively change your attitude and become more empowered.

"Between stimulus and response there is a space. In that space is our power to choose our response. In our response lies our growth and our freedom.", Viktor Frankl

Maintain great health

Diet, supplements and exercise are the best remedy to a long term solution of beating anxiety. So much research proves this. Again a healthy body equals a healthy mind and vice versa. Eat a well balanced and clean diet with lots of fresh fruit and vegetables. Have less processed food and more pure meats and so on. Exercise regularly and make sure it wears you out and works up a sweat. Try out some supplements. Omega 3 and zinc are two great ones for the brain.

Redirect your focus

Additionally you can redirect your focus away from anxiety to a new focus. Go and meet your friends for example. Or get involved in some enjoyable hobbies and activities. Here are some more examples to redirect your focus. Remember they should make you feel good or leave a sense of fulfillment.

- Clean the house or organize your workplace
- Do something creative such as writing or playing music
- Go out walking
- Do some sports or exercise
- Meditatie
- Enjoy listening to music
- Read an inspiring book
- Watch an inspiring movie

Aromatherapy and relaxation

Candles, scents and incense can be a really soothing relief to anxiety. Dim the lights and experience some aromatherapy. It will activate certain receptors in your brain to relax the anxiety. In addition you can put on some calming music. Stretch out and practice some yoga poses. Combine them with breathing and focusing on the present moment. Or you could meditate with the candles and aroma. Try this for just fifteen minutes a day or more and you will begin to feel much better.

How to manage depression

Finding the energy to take care of yourself and overcome depression can feel like a hard mountain to climb. That's why depression often lasts so long. It's almost easier to stay depressed than fight the beast. However it is possible to overcome and manage the condition. It won't be a magic pill or quick fix. Here's how to break through.

Push back

When you're depressed it's like a cloud of negative thoughts blocks your mind. Negative thoughts blur your vision. "I'm sick of this" "nothing ever goes my way" "How could I be so dumb". When you're in the whirlwind of those thoughts life can be unbearable. No wonder doing simple things becomes so hard. What you've got to do in those situations is to push back on those thoughts. Start questioning them and take a different point of view. Get up out of your chair and say no! Push back and come up with alternatives to those thoughts. It could be a rapid fire of attention. "I'm sick of this" becomes "I will beat this" or "I'm better than this" and so on. "Nothing ever goes my way" becomes "this won't last forever" or "soon the tides will turn my way, it's just a matter of time" and so on. You get the process. Now go ahead and push back.

Positive vibes

Depression episodes often bring back painful memories. Falling down that black hole of negative thoughts the depressed person is drawn further and further into the darkness. The dark feelings overwhelm them and the deeper they fall. But it doesn't need to be that way. Breakfree and pull yourself up. Force yourself to focus on a more positive memory. Think back on your life. What was your happiest memory? When did you feel happy recently? Go back to that memory. Visualize it. See what you saw, hear what you heard and feel what you felt. Take a moment or as long as you want to go deep into those happy memories. Anytime the darkness falls on you go back and visit those happy memories again. That will put a smile on your face.

Keep smiling. When people ask you how you're doing, tell them you're doing great. I know you're probably not and you prefer to be down but push back on that. Tell them something good. Take care of yourself. People with depression often neglect their health and basic hygiene. Make sure you keep up with showers, brushing teeth and practice good hygiene. In addition, eat a healthy diet and stick with regular exercise.

Make Plans

When you're feeling depressed your energy will be low. Tucked up under the bed covers feels like the best place to be. It's become easier and easier to live this way. Almost everything can be delivered right to your home so there isn't much need to go out or to make plans. But to overcome depression it's essential that you make an effort to make plans and fill your days. Get up in the morning, take a shower and get out there. Fill your days up. It will give you something to look forward to. Even scheduling a walk or mediation in there will give you more purpose and shift you away from depressive episodes.

Stay connected and find support

Social connection is directly related to inner well being and mental health. Problem with depression is that it causes us to withdraw. Much like pushing back on depression you need to stay connected socially. Confide in your friends and family. If they are not around schedule in a call with them. Even better if you can go meet them in real life. If you have a smaller social circle then join some online groups and forums. Step out of your comfort zone and join some meetups, sports clubs or even try volunteering. The chamber of commerce, toastmasters and dance classes are all very good general places to get connected with others.

Remember that depression doesn't have to define you. It is a common mental illness and one that can be treated. Remember to reach out for support and to take excellent care of your health. You're worth it.

How to manage information overload

Do you struggle to focus? Maybe your to-do list doesn't ever stop growing and it always feels like you're getting nowhere. Each day is a struggle in a cluttered world. Excessive mental clutter affects every area of your life. From how long it takes you to do things to how much pleasure you gain from life. It can distract you, weigh you down and bring chaos into your life. Faced with an avalanche of clutter, people freeze up and just don't know where or how to get started. Procrastination, doubt and overthinking clouds their minds. Oh there's always something more important or more interesting to be doing. Oh, how about that new series on Netflix. Or how about the new YouTube podcast, or calling your friend. All of these can be welcome distractions. Practiced in moderation they are fine. As long as you get done what you need to get done.

A mountain is climbed one step at a time and an avalanche begins with one snowflake. Both consist of many parts and steps. The same is true when it comes to decluttering your mind. With a little bit of time each and every day you can begin to gain an advantage over the clutter. Start to reap the rewards of a clutter free life. From reduced stress to more productivity and much, much more. The combination of small parts and steps build up to big efforts in the long run. Here's how.

Eliminate the nonessential and do more of what you love

The first step to dealing with information overload is to start reducing your commitments. Realize that the busier you become the more your life becomes cluttered. When you're feeling this way, take a look at the different areas of your life. Write out all the commitments that you currently have (this will be an eye opening experience). Ask yourself.

- Does it bring you joy?
- Does it add value?
- Is it worth your time?

These questions will help you to decide whether to continue with each commitment or to reduce how much time you spend on it or to drop it all together. Get comfortable with being able to say no and to politely decline opportunities. Make sure those are the right things for you or not. Be graceful. Eliminating the things that have less meaning to you will open up the door to doing more of what you love. In perspective from this point of view you can analyze each commitment and decide if it is bringing positivity to your life.

Plan your days

Take a look at your day to day life. We all have our own set ways and habits. But without structure our days can end up in chaos. Make a plan for your days. This is best done the evening before or first in the morning. Having that structure might seem like it's limiting you but it is actually freeing you because it keeps the mind from wandering off into negative thought patterns. It's a great exercise to write out your weekly and daily plans, appointments and routines. Have this written where you can see it and try to stick with it. Bring more calm and rationality to your life. No more being at the whim of negative influences and getting caught up doing meaningless things which will cause negative emotions such as guilt or shame later on.

Spend most of your time with positive people

This is going to sound cruel but you need to potentially stop seeing certain people in your life. Some friendships simply clutter your life. Instead, spend most of your time with positive people who make you happy and encourage you to grow. Sure some of those toxic friendships might be fun because you hang out, play video games and drink beers. A little bit of vice is fine but too much of it and it's not advancing your life. Therefore you need to move on. Maybe you need to get out there and make new friendships that are more positive. Consider taking up some hobbies, sports or solo traveling. All of these will put you into direct contact with ambitious and outgoing people. Those will result in positive and mutually beneficial friendships.

Become more organized

Clearing up the physical spaces you work and live in is an excellent exercise to increase productivity and reduce mental fog. Head to your office. Begin by clearing off your desk. Take literally everything off it and either store it or throw it out. Additionally give it a nice clean wipe down. Follow the same process for your living area. Clean out the piles of things, then wipe it down or brush it up. In fact you should be doing this weekly or even daily. Follow Jordan Peterson's advice and "tidy your room". Mind over clutter.

Taking things a step further it's a great idea to become even more organized and systematic. Try setting up an alphabetical filing system for each of your projects. The same can be done online with tools such as Trello and Monday.com. It's useful to label things and prioritize them. Schedule out your appointments using a calendar. Whilst you're on the computer get rid of any files or programs that you don't use. Clean up your emails, bookmarks and data. Reduce the number of subscriptions you have. Install some blocking software for websites that distract you. Make sure you do all of this regularly otherwise that clutter will once again build up and stress you out.

Remove any distractions

A famous study from the University of San Diego found that whenever you're distracted it triggers the fight or flight response in your brain. So each time there is a new notification on one of your devices it causes your train of thought to get lost. Start making an effort to remove any distractions that take away your focus. Close all browser tabs except the one you're working on. Uninstall applications during your work hours. Put your phone on silent. Turn off all notifications on any of your devices and put your phone away.

Naturally we will need a break after periods of working. But you should not just dive into a social media feed. That will just overload your mind. Instead try taking a short walk, listen to a soothing song or wander around your room. Set boundaries. When you become consistent with the processes of decluttering you're going to find you're feeling less stressed and more happy. Remember to begin small and stick with it daily.

Minimalism

Minimalism is a practice that can help you to become more free from overthinking and overload. In essence it is a tool to eliminate excess so that you can focus on what is important. As a result you will be living closer to fulfillment, happiness and freedom. A few of the other benefits include, more time for your passions, living in the moment, more creativity, better health, peace of mind and much more.

Now there is nothing wrong with owning some material possessions. That is completely normal. The problem is when it becomes out of control and just unnecessary. Fact is today's society owns too much stuff and gives too much meaning. We put owning that dream car or house above our health. We are willing to overwork ourselves in the pursuit of owning material possessions at the detriment of our health. We buy clothes to fit in with the crowd and align with the current fashion trends. But most material things don't give us lasting, deep happiness or fulfilment. The feeling it gives us is fleeting. Sure some of these things might be important to you. Having a basic level of comfort and confidence is awesome. Materialism is very useful for that.

The concept of minimalism will allow you to decide if certain material possessions are good for you or not. In turn it can help you to pursue a more purpose driven life. Nowadays that is more important than ever. There is an excess in the world, way too much noise and way too little meaning. Minimalism can help in getting rid of the non-essential so that you can focus on what really matters.

There is a common misconception about minimalism that it means to live like a monk with no possessions. No, to me that just sounds boring and sterile. Minimalism doesn't need to be like that at all. Basically it's about clearing away the non essential and unnecessary. Which in turn gives you more room for what you truly want plus more peace and time. You can take this as far as you want. From simply getting rid of a few things to living a basic, simple life.

So how do you get started with minimalist living? Begin with giving your house, room or apartment a good clean out. Get rid of all the clutter. Throw things out you no longer use. Those clothes you didn't wear for more than three months would be better off at a donation center instead of gathering dust in your wardrobe. Tidy up your desk. Tidy up your computer. Cut down your unnecessary appointments and identify where you are wasting time. You'll find all of this will leave you much lighter mentally. There are no set rules or one particular way to live minimally. In general it is to simplify living without unnecessary possessions and distractions.

How to make better decisions

Everyday we are presented with endless decisions to make. From what food to eat to bigger decisions such as who to marry or what company to work for. On and on the list goes. Because of so many choices and overthinking, many of us struggle with making decisions. We feel it's normal to think about decisions. But at what point does it become irrational to overthink decisions? Well of course that depends on the context. Indeed some decisions do require more thought. But it should always be a deliberate and active thought. Overthinking small decisions will just lead us astray.

The answer is to get comfortable making decisions. Sometimes our decisions might not work out how we want to. We have to learn to be ok with accepting and standing by our decisions whatever the outcome. In addition, reduce the number of decisions you need to make. Take a leaf out of Steve Jobs' book who wore the same style of clothing everyday. Or Barack Obama who wears only gray or blue suits. Such habits will help break you free from decision fatigue and give you more power to focus on the important things. Here are some more ways to overcome overthinking when making decisions.

Set a time limit on your decisions

Never rush yourself, but put a limit on the amount of time to make a decision. This will make you more effective and also improve your time management skills. Some big decisions you might want to sleep on or come back to later on so you can see if the situation has changed. Other decisions you shouldn't spend more than a few minutes on. Learn to prioritize and allocate the right amount of time for each decision.

Give yourself time to think

When presented with an important decision most people rarely give themself a chance to sit there with the decisions. Instead they fill their mind with other stuff such as scrolling social media or busying themselves with nonsense. Then they arrive at a bad decision. Not a smart way. Set aside time and be in the moment with just you and your mind to think on that decision. This is essential for big decisions. Use writing paper or a document to help you record your thoughts. Or go take a walk and reflect on it. Being in the present moment with the decisions will allow you to focus on what matters right now and to in turn make better decisions.

Use a decision model

There are some great models for making decisions out there. One method I recommend is to set up the options for a decision and then weight the value of each option. The scores of each option can then be tallied to present a clear winner. However, remember this will utilize cold logic. Take into account your gut and heart emotions. Again it is useful to be in the present moment or to limit the time when making the decision.

How to manage Insomnia

Instead of taking sleeping pills which often become addictive there are some natural ways to overcome insomnia overthinking. First of all try to stick to a regular time to go to bed and wake up. A window of seven to nine hours is optimal. So for example I go to bed at midnight and wake up at 8am. Choose times that work for you and try to get as close to those times as possible. If you miss those windows then you essentially missed a sleep cycle. A sleep cycle is around ninety minutes so just be aware of that. It could be another ninety minutes or more before the next window. Before you sleep try to wind down your screen time on devices. Around an hour before bedtime, let your mind relax. Try to meditate or journal so that your mind is more settled. Still if you can't sleep, don't try to fight it. Resist the urge to stimulate your mind with watching TV or looking at your phone. Try something more calming such as reading a book or listening to relaxing music. Avoid taking sleeping pills unless prescribed. People who take sleeping pills tend to build a tolerance to them. They end up relying on them and need them more and more. Better to stay natural.

How to manage medical conditions

If you have tried all of the above solutions in this chapter and none have helped you then maybe it's time to seek medical help. There are so many options. You could see a therapist or mental health professional who can get to the roots of your problem and help you to make a plan to overcome them. Why suffer more? Working with a counselor, therapist or medical professional will help you gain insights and find solutions. That could be therapy, medicine or more. Reach out to your health care provider before it's too late.

Now we have discovered some solutions to common causes of overthinking. It's now time to take a look at how we can deal with negative thoughts.

Freedom From Negative Thoughts & The Negative Bias

Imagine you're at a restaurant and the waiter gives you a mean look. How would you feel? Would you take it personally? Or would you think, "Oh maybe this guy is just having a bad day." Or are you the kind of person to take it personally and think something like "it must be because of me, I look so terrible today". Beware because those small things you take personally start to build up and it can disturb you for sustained periods of time. Negative thoughts linger.

According to leading psychologist and author Martin Seligman there are three primary causes of negative thoughts.

Overthinking

Fear of the Future

It's common for people to fear the unknown. In a future that has not yet happened it can be easy to imagine the worst case scenarios. Panic and worry are the result.

Anxiety About the Present

Typically people with low self-esteem and confidence worry what others think of them. Or they worry about whether they are doing a good job or not. Anxiety is the result.

Past regret

All of us have once done something we feel ashamed or embarrassed about. We are humans and none of us are perfect. Depression and shame are the result.

Negative thoughts can feel so real. They make us feel upset, anxious and worried. Life is no longer fun and the joy has been taken out. Like a bad taste it sticks in your mouth. It can even go as far as affecting your health. All that negative thinking leaves you sick and tired. No one wants this. So how do we deal with negative thoughts?

First and foremost realize that you do not have to accept them as reality. Next work on replacing your negative thoughts with thoughts that are more positive and that make you feel better. Think about it differently. For example if you're going through a tough time. You might think "I wish my life was like the good old days". Instead you could think about it like this. "This is a challenge now but I will get through it and my life will be better than ever before." This isn't about lying to yourself. All of what was said is true. Simply put you reframed it to be more motivating. Now that is a much more powerful way of thinking.

Are there any negative thoughts troubling you right now? Listen to your thoughts. Don't run away from them. Discover yourself. Maybe you find that you're being too hard on yourself or are having unnecessary negative thoughts. Come up with something more encouraging. After all you're the one who is in charge of your thoughts so get in the driver seat and take control.

Yes, and also take this seriously. Don't make the mistake of thinking these are just thoughts and that they are no big deal. Absolutely not. There is a strong connection between the mind and the body. Thoughts can directly affect your health. Positive thoughts cause your brain to release chemicals that can make your immune system stronger, lower blood pressure and improve overall health. As a direct result it makes you stronger and more resistant to illness. Plus you will feel much happier about your life. Let's take a look at some more solutions.

Simple ways to deal with negative thoughts

Acceptance and Commitment Therapy (ACT)

ACT is a method of reconfiguring your relationship to your thoughts. It works by defusing overthinking through exploring thoughts to gain control on them. Instead of trying to eliminate negative thinking ACT focuses on trying to change how we react to thoughts. The majority of human thought is random and can often be destructive. Thinking is a never ending mental stream, millions of thoughts are happening all the time and we are not fully able to control what thoughts arise. At best only five percent is meaningful and relevant. But we can control how we respond to them. Forming a new relationship with our thoughts can free us from the paralysis of negative thoughts.

Incidentally this way of reframing our thoughts has been around for a very long time. Buddhism and modern psychology was built on many of these concepts. You can find this practiced in mindfulness and cognitive therapy. Buddhist meditation instructs the student to become aware of their thoughts and observe them as consciousness. To not take them personally or push them away is a founding precept of the mediation practice.

The Buddha divided thoughts into two categories. There are wholesome thoughts which lead to peace and happiness. Then there are negative thoughts which lead to harm and stress. The mind dwells on its particular tendencies. If you're more sensitive to negative thinking then your mind will be more likely to end up in a negative state. But if you train your mind it can become more positive. To experience more happiness and inner peace work on becoming more observant and in control of your thinking.

Overthinking

Start to become open and curious to your thoughts as they arise. You don't need to believe in your thoughts or take action on them. Instead explore them with curiosity. Just like a psychologist would suggest you do. First notice your thoughts and investigate them. Especially any negative thoughts. Reflect on them and it will help to break their power.

Let's take a look at some examples of dealing with negative thought patterns. Imagine that you were just diagnosed with a serious illness. Maybe you tell yourself

"My life will never be the same" or "that's it for me".

Anything thinking like that is going to make you feel much worse than you already do. Why not work on becoming better? It begins in the mind. Try to reframe your thoughts to something like;

"Well this won't last forever, I will get better than before".

Don't hurt yourself twice. There are millions of stories out there of people overcoming the odds. Get inspired by them.

In addition to ACT I will offer you some more simple techniques to deal with negative thoughts. Realize that eliminating negative thoughts forever is unrealistic. As I mentioned it's human to feel sad or down sometimes. After all, it makes the highs in life that much better. Now a more realistic and sustainable way to manage negative things is to gain control of them. Changes won't happen overnight. It will require practice and commitment on a daily basis.

Challenge your negative thoughts

When a persistently negative thought arises, question it. Ask yourself at least five questions. You can use these examples and tailor them to suit you. Have them stored on your phone or somewhere with quick easy access. Even better if you can memorize them. Consider the following.

- Is this a true thought?
- Is this thought serving me or hurting me?
- Can I turn it into something positive or can I learn from it?

Overthinking

- What would my life be like without this thought?
- Is this thought hiding the truth from me about something that I am avoiding?

Focus on your feelings right now

Say that you feel sad at the moment. Focus on that sadness. But realize that the sadness isn't going to last forever. You're not doomed to feel this sadness forever. How long it lasts depends on how long you let it stay with you or when you decide to let it go.

When you find yourself in a state of overthinking take a moment to question whether your thoughts are coming from negativity or lack. Or are they coming from a more powerful place? Notice the thoughts of negativity creep up and start to spiral out of control as they gather speed. Recognize the patterns. The difference is that from negativity or lack the overthinking is not serving you. On the other hand if it comes from power then this is beneficial to you. The better you become at recognizing the patterns the easier it will become to tune into a more productive state of mind. Learn to recognize when your overthinking starts.

Socialize

All of us experience negative thoughts. Realize you're not the only one.

Confide in someone you trust. Share your feelings with them and open up. The more open, the more you gain. Good friends will comfort you and help you to gain new perspectives. Take time to enjoy life with your family and friends. We are social animals and it is in our nature to connect with others. It's well known that the people you spend the most time with end up influencing you the most. They will contribute to your habits and life choices. Spend most of your time with people you aspire to be like. If someone is a bad influence on you, have the courage to step away from them. Take time to grow a great social life. Join clubs, hobbies and get out there in the world. Socializing will also get you out of your head. Additionally it will give you a larger support network.

You're not in this alone. It doesn't have to be that way. Look at the most successful people.

Overthinking

Behind every successful person you will usually find countless mentors, support, friends and family who helped them get there. Even the tough Navy Seals have a team to back them up. You might think they got there alone but they were all helped.

'It is not true that I am self-made. Like everyone, to get to where I am, I stood on the shoulders of giants. My life was built on a foundation of parents, coaches, and teachers; of kind souls,' Arnold Schwarzenegger

'I get my knack for relationships from my mother,' Arianna Huffington

Find your support group and mentors. There are so many benefits. From overcoming your strengths to identifying your weaknesses and working towards success. Sometimes it can be something as simple as having a shoulder to cry on. Even if you think you're strong, fearless and can go it all alone it helps to have some support. Maintaining a positive mindset all the time is practically impossible. There will be times you feel weak and want to quit. With a support group they will help to push you back up.

Support groups and mentors are great. Sometimes we need the kick to fire us into action. Accountability is awesome for that. Maybe you have been slacking off. Your accountability group or partner will be responsible for getting you back on track. It's their duty to ensure you stick to your words and commitments. Find people with similar goals and visions. Agree to push each other along.

Health and Fun

The simple science of eating well, sleeping well and exercising has a direct effect on your mindset. As mentioned earlier the mind and body are closely connected. Therefore if you have a healthy body your mind will be healthy and vice versa. Join a gym and start a workout program. Or take up some sports. Go for walks. Once you're exercising right, remember to eat right. Consume the optimum amount of calories and nutrients for your goals. Don't go over or under. Make sure you eat plenty of fresh fruits and vegetables. Take vitamins, live long and be healthy. Many of us are our own worst enemies at times. Guilt or desire and shame make us work too hard and feel bad about ourselves. Rarely do we take time to reward ourselves, to sit back, enjoy life and play. Find something that makes you laugh. Have fun and enjoy life. Again and again I recommend great health because it is so super important!

Distraction

Distraction is a great remedy to overthinking. Have some hobbies that you can easily get involved in when you find yourself stuck in periods of overthinking. Maybe you play chess, cards or video games. It could even be getting up to stretch. Visualization is one of the most helpful and easy to implement distractions to negative thinking which you can use at any time and anyplace. When that negative thought arises, close your eyes and picture yourself doing something you love. That could be playing music, sports, partying with friends or making love and so on. Go through the images in detail and play them out in your mind. Give yourself at least thirty seconds to visualize that experience. Feel the feelings, see the images and hear the sounds. Make it a vivid experience. Over time your brain will become accustomed to switching from a negative to a positive situation.

Writing

Writing out your negative thoughts is a great way to throw them out of your mind. This will clear your head. You can use a pen and paper or even a laptop or phone notes. Remember that writing with pen and paper is proven to be more effective but on digital format is fine also. Depends on how bad your handwriting is or if you want to store it. Personally I like to store the notes and reflect on my progress years later. Whereas some like to write on paper and then burn it! What a great way to be released from your thoughts. Go crazy and write out all the bad stuff and be as honest with yourself as possible. No tricks or lies. Be truthful and make the most of it.

When you realize that negative thoughts are part of the mind and that you're not responsible for them it will help to break free from any attachment to them. The more we practice, shifting into our attention and thought patterns the more our mind begins to form strong and positive pathways. It takes time but it will be worth it in the long run.

A grateful mind cannot be a hateful mind. Positivity and negativity cannot occupy the same mind at the same time. Everyday there are millions of things to be grateful for. Become aware of them. Write them down. Think about them.

At this point we can realize how helpless negative thinking patterns can leave us feeling. Put an end to the suffering. Practicing the right technique is the breakaway that will effectively retrain your negative thinking habits. Now let's work on breaking those patterns with one more powerful way of dealing with negative thinking.

Cognitive Restructuring

Thought modification otherwise known as cognitive restructuring is a powerful yet simple technique that has been proven to treat various mental health issues including depression and anxiety. It is helpful for identifying and changing negative thinking patterns. In fact for anyone who struggles with negative thinking it can be a great remedy.

Thoughts and emotions happen automatically. Problem is when we are upset and in reaction then we are more likely to do stupid stuff that pacifies our feelings. For example we take drugs, drink beer, eat junk food or waste time procrastinating and so on. All of that can spiral out of control. Cognitive restructuring helps us to notice our bad mental habits and replace them with more positive ones. When we use cognitive restructuring it can help you to become more aware and in the moment. Simply put, it hands the power back to you. Instead of being something uncontrollable that just happens to you.

Think of the cognitive restructuring process as a way of organizing yourself mentally. Just like making a to-do list it helps you to be more organized and less overwhelmed. That's the premise of it all and that will allow you to have more brain power to focus on the important and bigger picture of your life. Negative thoughts are poison that comes with a corresponding negative emotion. If you can cut that out and reframe your thoughts then you will be much better off.

When we can learn to be consistent with this process (which takes time by the way), it will create a positive impact on every area of your life. Whenever that challenge or conflict comes up you can be more flexible in how you react to it. This will change how you think and feel about everything. Here are just some of the real world benefits of Cognitive Restructuring.

Become better at managing worry and anxiety

The mental habit of worry drives all anxiety issues. From obsessive compulsive disorder (OCD) to social anxiety and general anxiety disorder (GAD). Worry is caused when we irrationally expect unrealistic threats or dangers in the future. Even though there is a part of us that knows logically that these worries are irrational it is still a habit that is very hard to break. Cognitive Restructuring can be used to effectively identify the times when we engage in patterns of worrying. It can then help to replace it with more realistic and helpful thought patterns.

Break free from rumination and depression

Rumination is the mental process of continually going over past mistakes and turning them over and over again in your mind. This is always in a negative way. Whilst worry is about the future, rumination concerns thinking about the past. Similar to worry, being a key driver for anxiety rumination is also a key driver. In this case it is a key driver for depression.

Rumination can be difficult to break this habit. Just like worrying, it is a strong thinking pattern and it is addictive. People have become so used to it. Again Cognitive Restructuring can help to break rumination. This works by first of all identifying the depression genetairing thought patterns and then replacing them with something more positive and empowering.

Stress relief

The human mind is able to think, critically, analyze and evaluate. Such a unique and great strength. However without control it can also become a great weakness. For example if we are analyzing a conversation we had whilst trying to sleep then it is not very helpful. Ultimately patterns of thinking like this can lead to stress and burnout. Cognitive Restructuring can improve our ability to switch from a thinking and critical mind to a more relaxed one at the suitable time. This is a great way to handle stress as it comes up.

Overthinking

Stop procrastinating and become more productive

Becoming distracted from time to time is completely normal. Even putting things off or on hold for a period of time is normal too. However when we experience a wave of negative thinking about taking action is when it becomes problematic. Or when you never get anything done and those deadlines just pass you by. Maybe you have an endless list of tasks to do in your mind. Or maybe you're plagued by repeated criticism of yourself. The last thing anyone needs is a monkey on their back bothering them. That will just waste all of your energy.

Time passes us by. Most of that time is spent procrastinating. When we are faced with a difficult challenge we often waste tons of time avoiding it. We then tend to get busy with everything else but that. I know we are all guilty of that. Then we have the excuse that we are simply too busy. All these things we need to do again begin to pile up in our brain and constantly nag at us day and night. That is until you actually get them done or you delegate. Again all of this avoiding, indecision and procrastination are contributing factors to overthinking and mental anguish. The best solutions to avoid those avoidance coping mechanisms at all costs. Of course the best way is to just get on with it and do it. Right?

Cognitive Restructuring can effectively resolve procrastination problems. Through reprogramming our destructive thinking patterns it helps us to take action and get things done. Take a deep breath and get it done. Be decisive and take action right now. Take action now and get done what you have been procrastinating. It might seem unpleasant but you're probably blowing things up and out of proposition in your mind. Once you get that done you will feel so much better with it behind you. Tackle things one by one and gain massive momentum.

Better communication and relationships

Communication is the key to building and maintaining healthy relationships. We need to be able to express ourselves and listen with empathy. The same is true about how we talk to ourselves. If we constantly worry about offending others then it will be difficult to assert ourselves and achieve what we want from a relationship. Or if we constantly judge and are hard on ourselves then we will have trouble getting anywhere in life. Cognitive Restructuring can help to improve the way we talk to ourselves. As a result this will simultaneously improve our communication with others.

Increased Optimism

Sometimes it feels like there's just bad things going on everywhere in the world. But we don't need to have a pessimistic viewpoint. Sometimes you need to rise above it all and take the lead out. Cognitive Restructuring can help you to have a more optimistic view on life and a higher level of general happiness. Learning to examine and modify our habitual thinking patterns helps us to catch those overly negative or pessimistic thoughts. Many of those influences come from what is going on around you. Such as the news, media and so on. Turn those off and get in the control seat of your life.

Overcoming addiction

If you struggle with addictions then I know you understand how destructive your behaviours can be. Mindset and self talk play a key role in the root cause of addictions and their associated behaviours. If your goal is to make progress and break free from your addictions then Cognitive Restructuring can help you gain the mental mastery you will require to manage your cravings. When you gain control of your thoughts it extends into your behaviours which will in turn curb your addictive patterns. Simply it makes it easier to manage your thoughts and actions rather than them controlling you.

Increased confidence and assertiveness

Success in life depends on how well you can express the honest and true intentions of yourself in a respectful way. When we hold ourselves in high regard we start to believe in who we are and we pursue the goals we want. No matter how we feel on a given day we still persevere. Without confidence and assertiveness we are left at the side to fight for the scraps and a life that we don't really want. This just gets worse. Use Cognitive Restructuring to build a more powerful inner voice and witness the effects create an increased confidence.

"I hated every minute of training, but I said, 'Don't quit. Suffer now and live the rest of your life as a champion.'" It isn't the mountains

ahead to climb that wear you out; it's the pebble in your shoe.", Muhammid Ali

Cognitive Restructuring Steps

The fundamental principle of Cognitive Restructuring is based on cognitive mediation. This states that the way we feel in our emotions is not because of what has happened to us but rather it is the result of how we think about what has happened to us. For example, imagine you're at a party. You say hi to a stranger but they ignore you. Do you take it personally and negative self talk starts? Or maybe do you assume they are having a bad day or that they are just not on your vibe?

For the person who is more likely to take it personally and fall into a negative self-talk then you for sure you will benefit from Cognitive Restructuring. The process can be taken step by step. Together, let's take a look at those steps one by one.

Step 1, *Stop and reflect*

When you begin to feel a strong negative feeling instead of reacting to it, stop and reflect on it.

Have an attitude of curiosity. We can use our earlier example of the stranger at the party.

- Begin by thinking of the emotions you felt and the thoughts you had.
    - Ask yourself; What's going on here?

Step 2, *Identify the trigger*

What happened? You recognized a strong emotion inside of you. Your next step is to find out what triggered it. This could be something in the external environment such as a car cutting you off or in our example talking to a stranger who ignored you. It could even be an internal thought. To help identify the trigger;

Use; what, who, when, where questions?

- You talked to a stranger and he ignored you

Step 3, *Notice automatic thoughts*

What were your first thoughts? Our first thoughts are on autopilot. They are our default thoughts and are pretty much out of our control. All of us have automatic thoughts and most of the time we don't recognize them. Cognitive Restructuring teaches us to become more aware of them and examine them closely. In our example;

- You felt rejected.
    - Why did he ignore me?
        - Automatic thought
            - I must be a bad person because otherwise he would have been more friendly. Maybe I'm just a loser.

Step 4, *Identify your emotion and its intensity*

What were your first emotions? Mental interpretations of what happened create emotions. Each person's thinking causes different types and intensity of emotions. Say you have strong, angry reactions then of course you will be the type to get angry easily. Whereas if you experience thoughts of fear and worry then you will likely get anxious. In many cases you can get a mix of emotions often with one being more dominant.

- You felt sad and upset. Plus some sadness.
    - Rate it on a scale from 1-10

Step 5, Come up with alternative thoughts

Are there any alternative ways that you could think about what happened? Now that you have identified your trigger, automatic thoughts and emotions you can now work on restructuring them. First, come up with alternatives to your automatic thoughts. If someone cut you off in traffic instead of being angry, be grateful that they didn't crash into you. Come up with as many alternatives as possible. Those should disengage from negative thought patterns but also be realistic. Gratitude is great for this. Let's look at our earlier example.

- Maybe that guy was having a bad day.
- Maybe you didn't talk loudly enough and he didn't hear you.
- Maybe he is a bad guy and you're better off not knowing him anyway. Luckily we didn't talk.
- Feeling grateful.

Step 6, *Re-evaluate your emotional intensity*

How do you feel now? Alternatives to your automatic thoughts should lower your emotional intensity. The more realistic and believable they are the more effective they will be at reducing emotional intensity. Challenging, questioning and then reframing your thoughts and feelings will certainly make you less upset. Plus you're now in control.

Stick with the mental habit of Cognitive Restructuring. At first it will require a much more active approach. Commit to learning how to organize your thoughts and then modify them. The more you train your brain the stronger it gets at developing this new positive way of thinking. The rewards will make you want to stick with it as your negative feelings subside.

From now on whenever those negative thoughts come up, start the steps of cognitive restructuring or any of the previous techniques and tools. Try and test them all out. Then go with what works for you. That could change depending on the situation, your mood, causes and so on. Be flexible and adaptable. Now we have dealt with negativity. Now lets build up our armour in the next chapter. Let's take a look at it's opposite, positivity and how it helps you deal with overthinking.

Positivity

Positivity! Now I'm sure you've all heard that word before. But I guess it feels a little cheesy with all the self help gurus out there burning that word out. By definition, the root meaning of positivity is to think in an optimistic way. A way that expects successful results and focuses on being happier. In essence it is a happy and worry free state that focuses on the positives of life.

"Always look on the bright side of life", Monty Python

Is your glass half-empty or half-full? The answer to this will give you insights into your attitudes about yourself. It will help you to discover whether you're an optimistic or pessimistic person. Those very attitudes directly affect your health. Many studies have proven this. Optimism and positivity are essential to effectively managing stress. Naturally a less stressed out person is more healthy because they have lower blood pressure, less cortisol and free radicals messing up their health.

An optimistic person is more resilient to the swings of life. They don't take things personally. Worrying about the future or regretting the past doesn't bother them much. Instead of being consumed by overthinking they are able to focus on achievement and actually doing the things they enjoy. Negative feelings are diminsided and good feelings are the result. Positivity, love, joy, happiness and inspiration.

Don't get me wrong here. Being positive is not a state of ignorance. Maybe you've seen those people who at all costs try to avoid negative feelings. Like a forced smile, you can tell it's not authentic. Simply that's just burying your head in the sand and ignoring the challenges of life. Such thinking won't get you anywhere fast. True positivity does not try to avoid negative feelings. Instead it is completely aware of them. Power and growth comes in acknowledging them so that you can learn from them and work on becoming better. That will give you the courage to keep going when things get tough. Maybe you think that this is not for you. It seems so far off. But don't worry it can be achieved. Training your mind to become more positive is a real thing.

Scientific research continues to research how positive thinking affects health. So far they have found that it benefits some of the following.

- Longer life spans
- Reduced depression
- Lower stress levels
- Improved immunity
- Better physical health and well being
- Better heart health and less risk to cardiovascular disease
- Strong ability to endure stress and challenges

Positive thinking begins with correct self-talk

There is an endless stream of unspoken thoughts going on in everyone's heads all of the time. Those thoughts are automatic. They can be negative or they can be positive. If they tend to be more negative then you're likely to be more pessimistic. Whilst if your thoughts are mostly positive then you're more likely an optimist. In addition, positive and optimistic people usually live much healthier lifestyles. It's all a positive cycle of influence and all the habits stack up.

Life is an amazing and wonderful adventure. Instead of having a glass half full mentality we need to look on the bright side of life. Problem is that most of us tend to default to being negative. That's something that evolution installed into us. Our brains began as lizards and our natural flight or fight behaviours remain. Anger triggers us to attack or panic. So we tend to find ourselves still stuck in this thinking that we are going to be attacked by a predator. As much as we have advanced as humans, our biology still holds us back.

The human mind on a normal day can produce up to fifty thousand thoughts a day. Not surprisingly we can't control all of those thoughts. According to research almost seventy five percent of what we think is negative and works against us. To begin with, the odds are stacked against us! We know this from the previous chapter discussing the negativity bias. But just how can we possibly overcome this? What is required is a more deliberate and positive thinking.

Realize that positive thoughts aren't going to just appear in your mind. You need to actively take responsibility and engage in thinking positively. Remember how great you are and the amazing things you have achieved. Big yourself up and be grateful. This habit of going against the grain of your thinking can bring you back from despair and install confidence. Be kind to yourself. Dedicate some time each day to think positively. You can focus on recalling good memories or visualizing your goals.

Martin Seligman who is a leader in positive psychology is famous for saying "One of the most significant findings in psychology in the last twenty years is that individuals can choose the way they think." Additional studies from The University of Michigan concluded that organizations which have high performance rates are more likely to have leaders who make more positive statements. Those positive statements help to build stronger relationships. It's not about sucking up to someone. On the contrary you can be constructive in feedback and focus on building up someone's confidence. There are effective ways to implement positive statements. First of all make sure they are sincere and authentic. Remain objective in your evaluations both of yourself and of others..

Curate your own positive influences

The reality is that there is so much negativity in the world these days. Just turn on the news and you will be drip fed it all day long. The media and news know that this gets attention and so they push that narrative. Bad news gets views because it plays on our emotions of fear and anger. Those are very powerful emotions and when they are triggered they can grow like a snowball rolling down a mountain. Eventually this negativity spills over into our lives. But we have to be the gatekeepers of our minds and control what we allow into it. Otherwise it can slowly corrupt our minds. Resist this negative information. Curate your own positive influences. You don't need to know about murders and shocking crimes on the other side of the world.

Fill your mind with positive influences. It's up to you to make an effort to increase the positivity in your life whilst reducing the negativity. Take a look at how you're spending your time. What kinds of movies or TV do you watch? What kind of music do you listen to? Are those positive influences? Sure those sad songs can bring back memories of a lost love, but isn't it time to move on? Try something more uplifting. It won't resonate with you at first but give it a shot and stick with it.

Pay attention to what you are consuming. All of these influences might seem small but it all matters and it will all contribute to a more positive life. In addition to the media, pay attention to the mental images consuming your mind. The way you imagine yourself and your surroundings has an important influence on your thinking. Instead of dwelling on dark and negative thoughts, make an effort to focus on more colorful, light and uplifting thoughts. With enough persistence your mind will start to reject those unnecessary negative thoughts and welcome the positive ones. Remember that you become what you think about most of the time. Start thinking about great things and become someone amazing.

Keep a record of your thoughts and emotions. At the end of the day journal about them. What kinds of emotions and thoughts did you experience that day? Were they mostly positive? Or were they mostly negative? What caused those emotions? What can you do to make them more positive tomorrow? Remember positive thinking will improve your life and health!

Therefore the more you can fill your day with positive emotions the better your days will be.

Imagine your child once again

As I mentioned earlier it is possible to change your outlook on life from a negative to a positive. But it won't happen overnight. That's not real lasting change. No, I'm talking about achieving deep rooted, life lasting change. With daily practice and awareness this is possible. The journey goes on. Imagine your child once again. As children our thoughts are mostly positive. We loved to play and were free from doubts, fears or criticism of ourselves. Imagine how much you are limiting yourself now. Realize that you'll never live your dreams if you have those barriers made by yourself.

Break the barriers. Go after that job or relationship. Don't listen to those doubts that tell you you're not good enough. After all, you're a human on this earth and you deserve a shot as much as everyone else. Pump yourself up and take action. Doing that is not as hard as you think. You just have to do it. Replace those negative thoughts with positive ones. Be in the moment and take action. Action cures everything. You are more than enough. Better than you imagine!

Focus on the positive of every situation and don't take anything personally. Just because someone didn't smile at you. It means nothing. Maybe they are shy. Maybe they are having a bad day. Your inner dialogue is much different from theirs. Be curious, say hi. Take action and explore. Maybe it goes nowhere but you should be proud of yourself for making a move. The more you take action when your mind over thinks the more empowered, confident and positive you will become.

Gratitude

Become more grateful for the life you have. So much has been written about the positive effects of gratitude. Pay attention and make use of it. I like to wake up each morning and write out three things that I am grateful for. Following on I write out why I am grateful and how it makes me feel. Starting your days like this will develop your mind to be more grateful and set your day off on a positive note. Furthermore you can also do it at the end of the day. Write what you're grateful for that day.

Count your blessings. Instead of being frustrated with yourself try being grateful for recognizing your overthinking. It takes courage to do that. "I am grateful for feeling like this because it allows me to make a change".

When you become more grateful for life and yourself then your thoughts will become more positive. Your mind will be in a much more productive and happy state. Take a deep breath, relax and tune into gratitude.

Self-Esteem

Healthy and happy mental wellness results from a high level of self-esteem and in turn a greater quality of life. Self-esteem is a term used in psychology to describe the overall subjective sense of personal worth or value that a person has of themselves. In simpler terms it can be defined as how much a person likes themselves. This further defines a number of important factors including, confidence, identity, feeling of security, competencies and a sense of belonging. It plays a key role in overthinking. Low self-esteem is perhaps one of the most common reasons for overthinking.

Self-esteem fluctuates throughout our lives. In children it tends to be lowest and increases into adulthood before reaching a relatively stable level. Levels depend on the personality and lifestyle of a particular individual. For example influences that impact on it include, age, genetics, illness, physical ability, socioeconomic status, thinking and much more. Often our life experiences influence our overall levels of self-esteem. For example if we are surrounded by negative friends and family then we are likely to have low self-esteem.

When you begin to understand your own self-esteem it can help you to strike a well balanced life. Your relationships, emotional health and decisions are all influenced by self-esteem. That is why it is so important to create a positive view of yourself so that you are inspired by life and always rise to the challenge. Those with healthy levels of self-esteem are great at establishing and maintaining healthy relationships with others. This is because they already have a healthy relationship with themselves. In addition they are realists who understand themselves and can fully express how they feel.

On the other hand people who have low self-esteem tend to be much less confident in their abilities and often doubt themselves. As such they constantly struggle with motivation or trying new things because they lack enough belief in themselves. As a result their relationships suffer and they feel unloved or unworthy.

It's important to note that people can also have too much self-esteem. In that case they end up feeling entitled to certain success or achievements. Yet they don't have the abilities to back it up. Just imagine the trash talking boxer who gets knocked out. Yes, too much self-esteem will cloud your judgement and people will find it difficult to connect with you.

Causes of low self-esteem

As mentioned earlier self-esteem tends to be stable throughout a person's life. But it can change dramatically during your life. Difficult life experiences, stresses and challenges can cause such changes. Those might include.

- Someone abusing you or bullying you
- Prejudice or discrimination against you
- Losing your job or being unable to do your job

- Problems with work or study
- Overall life stress
- Health problems - mental or physical
- Problems with relationships
- Body image concerns
- Financial problems

There are various other reasons or experiences that might not be listed here. Just be aware of the negative vibes and bad influences in your own life. Whatever affects your self-esteem you should remember that it's right for you to still focus on feeling good about yourself. Change can be difficult but with small steps you make improvements.

How to have healthy self-esteem

When you have a healthier level of self-esteem you're going to be more motivated to go for what you want in life. You will also have the benefit of healthier relationships. Not just with others but also with yourself. Clearly having a higher self-esteem is a way to not only feel better about ourselves but also to become more resilient to overthinking.

Following on are some really simple ways to improve your self-esteem.

Feel confident or fake it till you make it

True you might not feel like a particularly happy person right now. Overthinking has it's hold on you and life just isn't going your way. When it rains ask, "is the best you have got to throw at me? Because I'm stronger!" Look on the positive side of things. Believe in yourself, no one is better or worse than you. We all have our own setbacks and version of life. Realize that you don't know what someone had to go through to get there and they don't know the same of you. So stop comparing. Believe it. If that seems so hard then just act confident and fake it until you feel it. Stick your head up and push your shoulders back. Stand up straight. Do things in a confident and calm manner. Take your time and don't rush things. Savour each moment and live it to the max. Change your behaviour and your thinking will change also.

Overthinking

Say no if you don't want to

Healthy self-esteem comes from strong values and boundaries. If you don't want to do something then say no. Problem is many of us take on too many responsibilities. We find it difficult to say no. Sometimes we just need to practice being able to say no or to delegate those tasks. Practice this skill. There are going to be times when you're asked to do something you prefer not to. Have the courage to say no. Trust me, you will get stronger with practice.

Stop dwelling on any past regrets or negative experiences

Be aware of your negative thoughts, identify them, challenge them and then change them. All of us have made mistakes in the past. The things we regret. The stupid things we said. The stupid things we did. But the past is in the past my friend and you cannot change it. Only can you change your perception of it. Instead of dwelling on the negatives of the past try to look at what you can learn. Switch from a victim to a victor.

Positive affirmations

Practice positive self talk. Try reciting affirmations to yourself. Affirmations have become very popular in recent times. But most are not really effective because they have a critical problem. That is they make people feel low self worth. This is due to the fact that the affirmations they use are too far from their existing beliefs. For example if your flat broke and you affirm that you're a millionaire then you're going to on some level realize it is just not true. Start where you're at and aim a bit higher. Be practical and make them believable. For example instead of saying "I'm a millionaire" you could say "I am on the path to riches". Or I am making "ten grand a month". Simply make them more believable.

Have a bunch of empowering affirmations that you can recite when you wake up and say before bed. In fact, say them whenever you feel like a nice boost. Keep at it and you will witness the results. Then you can keep on upgrading your affirmations as you fuel and grow your level of self-esteem.

Grow your strengths and work on your weaknesses

Self-esteem is grown by demonstrating your abilities and achievements. If you're good at something the more your belief in it grows. Figure out what your strengths are and do more of it. If you're a great cook then cook more. If you love lifting weights then do that more and so on. The confidence in your beliefs will spill over into your levels of self-esteem. All in all it's a positive building cycle. Do what you love and watch your self-esteem grow.

At the same time find what your weak areas are. Work on improving them. You can start small just like the first time you rode a bicycle. Then when you become more comfortable again your self-esteem grows. Be gentle and take it slow. Forgive yourself when you make a mistake. When it feels like you're not going anywhere, don't give up. Draw strength from your victories and keep growing.

Be your own best friend

When feeling bad about yourself it can be hard to accept a compliment. It feels like the person is joking with you. The next time someone compliments you, take it as a truth and be thankful for it. Prepare yourself in advance to thank them with words and a smile. Feel the emotions of praise. Stop judging yourself and being critical. If you were your own best friend you wouldn't behave in such a way. Start being your own best friend.

Improving your self-esteem will require some work. But in doing so you're building more healthy emotions and habits. The return on your investment will be worth it.

The Hierarchy of Needs

Abraham Maslow was famous for writing about the hierarchy of needs. Self-esteem plays an important role in the hierarchy of needs. It is one of the most basic of human motivations and is found at level four of the hierarchy of needs. We need appreciation from others and self respect in order to experience healthy self-esteem. In turn both needs must be satisfied in order for us to reach the highest level of self-actualization.

The hierarchy of needs explains that human motivation is based on pursuing different levels of needs. Those needs are set in a hierarchical order which humans are intrinsically motivated by. The order begins with covering the most basic of needs before moving on to more advanced needs.

Level 1: Physiological Needs

Physiological needs are at the bottom level of the hierarchy of needs. These concern the essentials of human survival. Those are things such as the need for water, food, shelter, rest health and so on. A person is motivated by this level in order to survive.

Level 2: Safety Needs

Safety needs are at the second level of the hierarchy of needs. A person needs to feel safe and secure within their environment. The motivation for law and order comes from unpredictable and dangerous conditions. People need protection from the elements, violence, sickness and so on. They also need job security, savings and income.

Level 3: Love and Belonging Needs

Love and Belonging needs are at the second level of the hierarchy of needs. Humans are social beings that feed off of interaction with others. We all need friendships, family and love. Our desire is to feel wanted and to give love. Without it we might experience depression or loneliness.

Level 4: Self-Esteem Needs

Self-Esteem needs are at the second level of the hierarchy of needs. Those are related to the human need to gain status, respect and recognition. With love and belonging needs fulfilled we seek to fulfill our self-esteem needs. This can be broken into two categories. The need for others' respect and the need for self respect. The respect from others concerns concepts such as recognition, fame, prestige, and so on. Whilst self respect needs concerns to confidence, dignity, competence, freedom and so on.

Level 5: Self-Actualization Needs

The final level of the hierarchy of needs is self-actualization needs. This is when an individual reaches their full potential. At this level they become the best version of themselves. This can manifest in ways such as education, skills development, fulfilling life dreams, pursuing happiness, love and so on. It could even mean becoming the best parent or a best friend. In general it is the pursuit of excellence.

Now we have explored the perils of negativity and washed ourselves with positivity. Arriving at this point we have a fairly clean slate or new foundation to build up our minds. Let's now look at some powerful tools and mindsets in the next chapters.

Thomas Swain

Meditation & Mindfulness

Meditation

Meditation as it is most commonly known is the practice of training attention. Most people assume that meditation is something practiced in a temple with a monk sat cross legged on a cushion. But it doesn't have to be that way. It can be as simple as a state of mind. For example, when we are doing something we give it our full attention in the moment. Washing the dishes can be a mediation. Walking can be a meditation. Mainstream practices involve taking the time out to sit down, close your eyes and focus on your breathing as it goes in and out. Inevitably thoughts will arise, but as you notice yourself getting distracted by them you gently bring your attention back to your breathing.

Overthinking

Mediation has been proven again and again by countless studies that conclude it improves focus and brain function. All you need is ten minutes a day and you can begin to reap the rewards almost immediately. The amazing thing about mediation is that it spills over into your daily living. After some weeks of daily meditation you will start to notice that food tastes better, you see more clearly and life is less stressful. This is because meditation is calming down your internal dialogue and allowing you to be in the moment experiencing life at its fullest.

Mediation has grown in popularity over the last few decades. What was once just something practiced by monks has now become a commercial success. Meditation groups have surged in popularity and even the business world has picked up on it. Of course meditation isn't some magic pill that cures everything in your life. But it will provide some much needed space. Here are some excellent reasons to meditate.

- Self awareness
- Stress relief
- Connect with life
- Better focus

- Less brain chatter

Meditation and overthinking

Overthinking takes over your mind and can lead to doubt, suspicion, and overall bad mind states. Overthinking is a big issue for many of us. We admire thinkers such as Shakespeare, Darwin and Einstein who have changed the world with their thinking. That type of thinking is a positive trait but overthinking is not. Essentially overthinking is a tidal wave of random unhelpful thoughts. Now that won't help you or bring you peace. However, meditation is something that can help to resolve overthinking and bring peace to your life.

Meditation can help you to gain perspective and see the larger picture of life. In turn that leads to a more peaceful and happy life. Seeking out a higher state of consciousness will help you to overcome your negative thoughts and declutter your mind. Dealing with life in a more organized and calm way without getting distracted from your purpose and happiness. Plus you will be free from attachment. So many benefits.

Meditation and the brain

In 2005 Sara Lazar, a Harvard neuroscientist published some astonishing research about mediation. She found that meditation can literally change the brain structure by thickening parts of the cortex that are responsible for controlling attention and emotion. In a little as eight weeks of practicing, daily half hour meditation this brain change is possible.

Further studies in 2014 found that the brains of meditators had enlarged regions. Those included the insula which is responsible for emotional self-awareness and also parts of the cingulate cortex, orbitofrontal cortex and prefrontal cortex. These are responsible for self-regulation and attention. It is no wonder that experienced meditators are better at focusing and struggle less with stress, worry, anxiety or overthinking. Various other studies have proven that meditation can change our neural circuitry which makes us more compassionate and more likely to experience positive feelings.

Not only does meditation change internal emotional states as a result it also changes our behaviour. One study in particular concluded that people after being trained in mediation for just two weeks were more likely to make charitable donations. Whilst another study discovered that people who meditated are more likely to offer a chair to someone who needs it.

There are five regions of the brain associated with healthy function which are substantially affected by meditation.

The Left Hippocampus

This area of the brain is responsible for helping us to learn. Cognitive ability and memory are found here in addition to emotional regulators that are responsible for empathy and self-awareness. Various research has concluded that the cortical thickness of this area grows when a person mediaites daily. As the density increases those important functions are improved.

The Posterior Cingulate

This area of the brain is associated with self relevance and wandering thoughts. It considers how one subjectively refers to oneself as they process information. The stronger and larger this is the less the mind will tend to wonder. In turn the more realistic a sense of self will be.

Since meditation trains the mind to remain in the present moment it directly benefits the posterior cingulate which increases its density.

The Pons

This area of the brain is a very busy and important part that hosts many neurotransmitters which regulate brain activity. It can be found in the middle of the brain stem and that's where the name pons comes from which is the Latin word for "bridge." A number of essential brain functions are attributed to the pons. Those include facial expressions, sleep, physical function, sensory input and more. Meditation has been found to strengthen the pons.

The Temporo Parietal Junction (TPJ)

The TPJ is associated with compassion, empathy and our sense of perspective. Whilst the posterior cingulate focuses on "me", the TPJ focuses on everything else. When we consider things from another perspective The TPJ becomes more active. The benefits of meditation such as lowering stress, anxiety and putting us more in the present moment combine to create a stronger TPJ. This can help us to become better people since we have improved empathy and compassion.

The Amygdala

This area of the brain is responsible for producing anxiety, fear and stress. This is the threat detection area of the brain. When it perceives a potential threat it will trigger or fight or flight response. This then releases the stress hormones which include cortisol and adrenaline. This causes us to get fixated on the threat and make it hard for us to break free and focus on anything else. In the brains of meditators it is physically smaller. Reducing this size is great because as a result we are going to be less sensitive to negative emotions. It's no wonder we feel better with a daily dose of meditation.

In a 2012 study people who had never mediated before were trained for eight weeks of mediation. Before they started the training they had MRIs, scans to discover where their brain activity was occurring. Whilst they were being scanned they were shown upsetting images. After the eight weeks of meditation training they were shown those images again whilst under the MRI scanner. This time their brain activity showed a reduction in the amygdala. One of the most amazing things about the 2012 study was that the reduction of amygdala activity continued even when the participants went back to their baseline state. This further proves that meditation can result in lasting mental changes.

How to Meditate

Now with all that being said one more thing needs to be explained. You won't change your brain unless you sit down and do your daily meditation! Sure some days you won't want to. Everything else is way more important. Push on and stick with it, even on the bad days. The practice is very straightforward and easy to do.

To begin with, find a comfortable place to sit and relax. It should be free from distraction and comfortable. You can choose to lie down or sit as you please. The best results tend to be seated cross legged. Strike a balance between alert and comfortable. Choose a time that works for you. At the start of the day or in the evening are the best times. Set a timer for ten minutes at first.

As you become more comfortable with the mediation you can build up to longer sessions

Setting aside a time each day is an effective way to establish a consistent meditation routine. With daily practice you will become more accustomed and comfortable with that practice. All it requires is just a few minutes a day. That can make a huge difference in your day to day life. I know we all have busy lives and it does require taking time out of your day. But the busier you are the more important it is. With mediation you will become a more effective person because it will stimulare long lasting benefits into our lives. From reduced stress levels, awareness with ourselves and greater connection with life.

So how do you actually mediate? There are many ways to meditite. Most of those are beyond the scope of this book. But here I will outline a simple mindfulness meditation. Primarily this is about learning to focus on your breathing. As each breath goes in and out, notice how your mind tends to wander from the task. The muscles of mindfulness and attention are built by practicing returning your focus to your breathing. When you learn to pay atten to

Overthinking

your breathing it anchors you into the present moment. Here and now without judgement.

It sounds simple and easy to do but it requires patience and discipline. Our minds have been burned out by all the distractions and information nowadays that something so simple has become so challenging.

Follow this step by step process to meditate

Step one

Find a comfortable place to sit. You should strike a balance between comfort and alertness. Laying down would be too much comfort. You might fall asleep. Whilst standing would be too alert and not enough comfort. Sitting on a seat or cross legged on a cushion is good. You can do this with eyes closed or open. Go with what gives you the most present feeling.

Step two

Set a time. In the beginning you can set an alarm to go off after five to ten minutes. As you get more comfortable and experienced, try longer times. Twenty minutes is optimal. Oh and remember to turn your phone off and make sure you have no other distractions. Start the timer.

Step three

Notice your body. Scan your attention across your body and pay attention to each area. Move around if you need to at first to make sure you're comfortable. Then stay in that position.

Step four

Focus on your breathing. Begin by counting to ten and focusing on your breathing. Follow the sensations of your breathing as each breath goes in and out. Notice all of the smallest details from the air filling your lungs to passing your lips. You will notice moments of pure presence. That is pure consciousness. You will know when it happens. No thinking just in the moment.

Let go and just be with your breathing. Thoughts will run through your mind but when you catch yourself caught up in them forgive yourself and return to focusing on your breathing. Allow your mind to relax into the moment and experience consciousness.

Overthinking

Step five

Notice anytime your mind wanders from focusing on your breathing. This is natural and will inevitably happen. When you notice this has happened forgive yourself and thank yourself that you are coming back to the present moment. Return your attention to your breathing. Don't be hard on yourself for it. Simply return back to your breathing.

Step six

When the timer goes off gently open your eyes if they are closed. Stretch your body and take a moment to notice your environment, thoughts and emotions. Give thanks for the moment.

As you can see meditation is pretty simple to do. The best results come from committing to doing it everyday. No days off. Even when you do not feel like doing it, stick with it. It's a beautiful thing and the more you practice the more you will fall in love with it.

Walking meditation

Walking meditation is another great meditation practice. Find a place that has plenty of space.

It's great if the floor has lots of texture to it. Remove your shoes so that you can feel the details of the floor in your feet. Begin to walk slowly. With each step focus on the experience of walking and the sensations it brings. When you reach the end of your path, start again until you have completed the time you want to meditate.

*Important: Remind yourself to meditate

Make meditation a part of your morning or evening routine. I personally practice after reading in the morning. This works because I stack my habits. Doing one habit triggers a cue to do the next and so on. In the evenings I also meditate. My cue is arriving home or taking an evening shower. Then I meditate and journal after. Use physical reminders such as a yoga mat or a cushion in your room. Put reminders on your phone or even stick up post notes in your home. Everytime you see any of those it will remind you to meditate. Stick with it.

Mindfulness

Scientists estimate that up to ninety five percent of human behaviour is on autopilot. Functioning in such a hectic world relies on habitual behaviours. Shortcuts established in the neural networks of our brains help us complete various activities on autopilot. Problem is our brain might sometimes think it knows what is best for us which can cause us to relapse into bad behaviours. But as discussed earlier in this book much of that is coming from our primitive brain. We need to get back in the driver seat. Our intention must be stronger and we need control to achieve that.

Mindfulness is a powerful method of counteracting this primitive type of thinking. It is the opposite of autopilot behaviour. Instead it is direct control of your actions and decisions. But it's not something that comes easily. The process will require you to rewire your brain from mental clutter of the past or future and to instead focus on the present moment. This is a mode of behavior that requires practice to activate our brains and make them stronger. With practice we stimulate our brains neuroplasticity and activate grey matter. In turn new neurons are formed and stronger pathways are built.

Truly it is a simple but incredibly powerful concept that can be utilized at any time. From during the most mundane of activities to during the most thrilling. In a mindful state you will no longer be attached to or be a victim of your thoughts. The result is simply being present in whatever you're doing at that time and experiencing it fully. Building the habit is what is challenging. However if you're willing to make a change and start practicing mindfulness then it will become easier to adopt this new concept. There are also some key habits you can utilize to welcome a more mindful state.

First you need to be prepared to have an open mind to new suggestions. Such new ideas will require change to defeat those bad habits which are creating chaos and confusion in your mind. Make an effort to regularly spend time cleaning your mind of overwhelming or obsessive thoughts. Otherwise those thoughts can linger around in your mind and negatively affect your emotions. Are you ready to clear away brain fog and reduce the noise of mental chatter?

How to practice mindfulness

Practicing mindfulness is all about directing your attention to the details of daily life. It won't require you to take a class or sit in uncomfortable positions for hours. Everything you have is already within you right now. Instead of being stressed out or anxious we take time to enjoy each moment and sensation of the moment. Turn the volume of your mind down and bring your awareness back to your body.

"Mindfulness is awareness that arises through paying attention, on purpose, in the present moment, non-judgmentally," Jon Kabat-Zinn, creator of the program Mindfulness-Based Stress Reduction (MBSR)

Just like a seed grows when watered, mindfulness also grows through the water of consistent practice. Regular practice will help you to overcome overthinking and break free from negative emotions. Set aside time each day to be mindful. Every moment you have it is available to you. It can be as simple as scanning your body or breathwork.

Body scan

A body scan involves you paying attention to each part of your body from your head to toes. Take a moment. You could be sitting in traffic. Focus. Begin at the point of your toes. Bring your awareness to them. Shift to your heels, then to your ankles, lower legs and up to the top of your head. Notice and pay awareness to each part.

It can help to lay down on your back. Have your legs laid out in front of you and arms at the sides with the palms faced upwards. Start to focus your attention onto the individual parts of your body. Go slowly and deliberately. Become aware of the sensations, thoughts and emotions associated with each body part.

Meditation

Mediation is the ultimate practice of mindfulness. Setting aside time to practice consistently each day will naturally make you more mindful. It's like a byproduct of the mediation. You become more mindful during each day. Try out seated or walking meditation. For more information on practicing meditation see the earlier part of this chapter.

Breathwork

Breathing triggers the parasympathetic nervous system which results in more calmness. Similar to meditation, breathwork or conscious breathing is another tool we can use to ground ourselves. Take deep measured breaths into your diaphragm. Count them as they go in and out. This lowers your stress and anxiety. Next time you feel stressed out, start doing some deep breathing. Focus completely on the details of your breathing. As it enters your body and exhales. Count all the way. Allow your breathing to bring peace back to you.

Remember that mindfulness isn't about silencing your mind. The goal is to become aware of the present moment without judgement. It's natural to make judgements as situations and events arise. When you become aware just make a mental note and let them pass you by like leaves in the wind. Stay in the present moment and just observe. Your mind will try to carry you away in the wind but you stay grounded in the present. Whenever your mind begins to wander, practice recognizing when it happens. Forgive yourself if you get distracted. It's normal, just gently come back to the present moment.

Take the time to enjoy the experience of life. Immerse yourself in the moment. When you touch, see, smell and taste. Take the time to enjoy it all and live fully in the moment. You'll find there is so much joy to be found even in the simplest of pleasures. The more you practice mindfulness the stronger it gets. Think of it as connecting with and taking care of yourself.

Now let's explore some more techniques, tactics and minstates to deal with overthinking.

More Techniques, Tactics & Mindsets

Finally you have some time out to yourself. Only then your mind starts overthinking! What about that email I was supposed to send? Why did I say that to her? What should I wear tomorrow? Does any of this sound familiar? Forgive yourself because it's all part of the experience of being a human.

Train your brain. Retrain it to think differently with the correct practices. When you pay attention to your thinking it will help you to become aware of any bad mental habits. Through building healthier habits you will build stronger mental muscles to become a better person and one who is more free from overthinking. In this chapter I will give you some more techniques, tactics and mindsets that can help to deal with your overthinking.

Self awareness

Realize when you're overthinking. For some of us this might prove to be difficult because it has become so normal. Self awareness is one of the most important ways to change your mindset. The next time you find yourself overthinking take a step back and become aware of it.

"We suffer more in imagination than in reality", Lucius Annaeus Seneca

Close your eyes and take a deep breath. Become aware of your feelings, thoughts and emotions. This is the first step you need to take. Now that you're self aware you can focus on cooling down. Find a comfortable place. Turn off any distracting or stimulating things. If there is music on, switch it off or put on something more chilled out. Turn your phone data off. In fact, get away from any screens. Going outside into some nature would be ideal. Maybe sit down in the park or go for a walk outside. Pay attention to your body. Relax your posture. Breath deeply in and slowly out. Stay here in the present moment. Again meditation, prayer and mindfulness can help you stimulate this.

Stop trying to fight your thoughts. This may sound counterintuitive but the effective way to really stop persistent unwanted thoughts is to first observe them in a curious and non-judgmental way. This alone may help to decrease their intensity. For example if I told you not to think of a pink elephant you're probably going to think of one. The same is true with those persistent thoughts. When you try to stop them it usually makes it worse. Just allow them, and they will dissipate eventually.

Be kind

Be a kind person. Empathy and thinking from another perspective will help you greatly here. If your overthinking stems from interactions or thoughts of other people then it can be a great idea to first of all think about things from the other person's perspective. How we see the world is shaped by our own values, assumptions and life experiences. When you imagine that view point from someone else it can help you to break through mental noise.

The world is a huge place and most people are focused on their own journey. The truth is they probably are not really thinking that much about you. But we have become so reliant on the opinions of others. We are willing to spend so much time thinking about how much they value our self worth or if they approve of us. It's almost as if our identity has become no longer a reflection of ourselves but rather a conformity to others. Our fears trick us into thinking things and opinions don't exist.

Do nice things for other people. When you see the opportunity to help others, do it. It doesn't have to be any grand gestures. Every little helps. Send those ripples of kindness out into the world. Maybe your neighbour needs a lift. Give that stranger a smile. Tip the waiter. Pick up some trash. Be sincere in your efforts.

Remember to also be kind to yourself as well. Dwelling on past mistakes won't help. Stop beating yourself up, learn and let go. If you need a friend to talk to then reach out to your social circle, family or even a qualified therapist.

Questions

Let your thoughts have their voice. Listen to them. Once you have heard them, begin to question them. Ask yourself;

- Is this helping me?
- What would be a better way to think?
- What are the consequences?
- Is there a better solution?
- If this were my last day on earth would I think like this?

Have these questions written out. There was a time in my life when I was plagued by overthinking. To retrain my brain I had lists of questions written out on my phone. Whenever I was faced with a long period of time to myself I would read them over one by one and answer each. Usually I would do this aloud. It truly reframed my thinking to become more constructive.

These questions were gathered over time and it took me about thirty to sixty minutes to go over all of them. I used to work a night shift and during the last hour I had almost nothing to do. Typically my mind would start going into depressed negative thinking as a default.

Because life is like a slippery slope and the devil is always grabbing at your ankles. You have to keep pushing up or it will drag you down. So at that time I decided to take hold of the reins of my destiny. The questions I had were all conducive to state changing. They had to have that effect. I would Google for questions to ask yourself or state changing questions. Things like that. You will find tons of those "fifty questions to ask yourself" and so on. I saved any that resonated with me. They had to inspire me. They would also have a follow up question. For each area of my life I had questions. For example,

- What am I proud of? What about that makes me proud?
- How is this situation making me stronger? How is that going to make me feel?
- Who do I love? Who loves me?
- How do I want to wake up feeling? Why?
- What's the best way to spend my time? How could I make it better?

Focus on solutions. Questions will give you the solutions. Dwelling on your problems will not help you. It can be easy to get carried away with negative thoughts. Take responsibility.

Think Big

The Magic Art of Thinking Big is a world famous classic book. One of the most useful messages in that book is to take time out each day to Think Big. Some of the most powerful and influential people in the world are known for practicing this. From presidents to billionaires to athletes. Time for reflection is essential to their development and success.

Instead of stewing on your problems, take time to focus on thinking of solutions. Use your questions to get your thinking going in the right direction. Block off at least thirty minutes a day to just sit down and think big. There should be no diastricons present. No phone or technology. You could go for a walk and do this. Sometimes your mind just needs to unwind and rewire itself a little. Kind of like formatting a hard drive. Sometimes you might want to think of a particular goal or challenge you are facing. Think about it from different angles. Or sometimes you can think big about your future and how you plan to succeed.

Think of the big picture. For the most part overthinking is a great big mess of small and meaningless thoughts. When you catch yourself overthinking, consider the bigger picture. How will these thoughts and issues affect you in the next five to ten years? Will they really matter? I doubt it. So therefore don't waste too much mental energy on them.

Think big and prime your brain to become more powerful. The human brain is incredibly adaptive. It can learn to adapt to new challenges and ways of thinking. This can happen incredibly fast. The act of taking time to think constructively will prime your brain to become more powerful. Use it to your advantage and unlock your full potential.

Distraction

The lure of overthinking can be so strong. Research has shown that distraction can help us to break free from overthinking. Choose activities that are highly engaging and positive; it can be a strong remedy. Good examples include puzzles, vigorous exercise, dancing or playing a strategic game. Those will be effective at shifting your attention from overthinking.

Most people associate distraction with being something negative but it can be a healthy distraction such as going to play sports, gardening or going for a walk and so on. Replace overthinking with an activity that you enjoy. Be in the moment with the activity. That could be anything from cooking to exercise to making love. Or it could be getting up and going for a walk. It could even be something within your mind such as replaying a great memory. The key is to find distractions that are positive and put you in the present moment.

Philosophical razors

In philosophy there are principles known as razors which can help you to shave off any bad thinking. Two major philosophical razors provide wisdom to avoid overthinking.

Occam's razor

The principle of Occam's razor states that when there are two explanations for an event the simple one is the most likely cause. For example when you have to make more assumptions the more unlikely a reason becomes. This can help you to overcome overthinking that comes from past fears.

Hanlon's razor

The principle of Hanlon's razor steam from Occam's razor. This suggests that avoiding any assumption of wrong intentions, stupidity, incompetence, or error could explain the cause. Therefore any chances of an event happening because of bad intentions are far less likely. Understanding this will help you to stop get caught up in overthinking caused by the assumption of bad intentions.

Change your stories

Tony Robbins is one of the most famous self help gurus ever. This particular method was

Overthinking

suggested by the man himself. Our mind is full of stories that we choose to tell about ourselves. For example, your date is twenty minutes late and she hasn't replied to your messages. You can tell yourself any of the following examples of stories:

She isn't coming
Or
She probably go delayed

Or another example. Your boss didn't respond to your email about a potential raise. You can tell yourself any of the following examples of stories:

He isn't going to give me a raise
Or
Maybe he didn't have time to reply

It's up to you to change your stories so that they are more positive and stop you from overthinking. Until you do that you're more likely to fall into panic attacks, anxiety and overthinking. Instead why not manage your stories? Think about it. Do your stories empower you or hold you back? Maybe you tell yourself that

"I always worry too much"
Or
"I'm not good enough"

To overcome these stories and beliefs you first of all need to identify them. When these scenarios come up, write down the first thoughts you have. Notice that there will be themes popping up. Start working on replacing them with more positive and empowering stories. When you change your story your life will change for the better.

Exercise

Exercising is an excellent way of countering stress, anxiety and overthinking before it happens. Healthy body equals a healthy mind and vice versa. I have pushed this many times in this book because of its high importance. Exercise gives us a welcome distraction or break from overthinking. Take the time out each day to practice some physical exercise. It should be challenging enough to keep you engaged but not too challenging to put you off. You should feel like you're making progress whilst gaining a healthier body. There are so many videos on

YouTube to learn about exercising. Or you could join a local fitness club or gym.

Go out into nature or for a walk. When your mind won't stop and overthinking is driving you crazy, step outside into nature or go for a walk. It will help you to restore mental clarity and gain a new perspective. If you're out in nature you will be humbled and inspired by the beauty. Your overthinking will subside as you take in your surroundings. Try to go for daily walks and if you can't look at some pictures of nature. Let it inspire you. Stay active and healthy. In addition, eat a healthy, clean and nutritional diet. This will optimize the functions of your body since they are provided with quality fuel.

Journaling

The Harvard Medical School studied the effects of expressive writing (journaling thoughts and emotions) and they found that it can effectively clear your mind. Simply put it is a way of expressing yourself through writing. Think of it like talking to a friend. This is highly effective at making sense of and processing your thoughts. Having them written out relieves your mind. In addition it will help you to organize your thoughts and understand your emotions. It makes complete sense to add this to your daily routine. All it requires is five minutes. Journal about your day or anything that bothers you. Think of it as a mental brain dump.

If there are thoughts swirling around in your head, write them down. Investigate each one and question how true they are. Journaling is an excellent relaxation exercise that will also give you valuable insights. Identify and record your thoughts in your journal. Actively work on trying to change them for the better. Get to the root of the cause of any bad feelings. Use your notebook to help you search inside. When you dig into the details and evaluate your thinking you can work on making a positive change.

Every day we are inundated with information and we need to take time out to process it. If something has been stuck in your head, get it out onto the paper. Free your mind. Do this without judging yourself. You're the only one who is going to read it and so it doesn't need to be grammatically correct or flow like Shakespeare. At the end of the week you can go over your notes, review them and gain strength.

I'm sure over time you will notice recurring themes. Take action on those.

In addition to tracking your negative thoughts, be sure to also acknowledge your successes. Praise yourself when you do something well. Write out the things you did well and what you're grateful for. It doesn't have to be something huge. Simple things. Let them add up.

Set goals and stick to them

Life is here for you. Why not live it to the fullest? Dare to dream. What would you like to achieve in this life? Where do you see yourself in five years? How do you want to feel? What kind of relationship would you like to have? How much money do you want to make? What kind of experiences do you want to have? Ask yourself questions to find out what your goals are. Set goals for the near future in say one month, goals for mid term in say six months to one year and long term goals for five years or more. Stack the importance and make plans to achieve them.

Having clearly defined goals with plans will reduce overthinking. Since you know what your purpose and goals are it will mean you're less likely to get distracted or caught up in overthinking. Have your goals written out and everyday check them. I personally have a spreadsheet of them and in addition every morning I write them out. It takes less than ten minutes but it puts my mind into the right focus. The reticular activating system (RAS) is a set of nerves within our brain which serves to filter out unnecessary information allowing only the important through. It is the reason why when you learn a new word you begin to hear it everywhere. Or when someone says your name in a crowd your attention immediately snaps to it.

With clearly defined goals we are more likely to stay on track and do the right things. Our RAS ensures that. Have lists of your goals and the actions you need to take each day, week, month, year and so on. Be organized and purposeful. Having this kind of meaning to your life will reduce the amount of overwhelm and overthinking since most of it will not matter. Peace and focus will become your new midstates now that you have purpose.

Mental Toughness

When thinking of mental toughness you probably imagine a navy seal or commander fearless and stoic. Essentially, mental toughness is a positive set of mental attributes that help a person to deal with challenging situations. In short it is a person's ability to resist, deal with and overcome any worries, overthinking, doubts or concerns that are preventing success. Of course this is a great remedy for overthinking. Those with mental toughness are much less likely to engage in self doubt, worry or overthinking.

The concept of mental toughness originated from sports training and psychology to help elite athletes perform better. The studies emerged in the mid 1980s and have continued to this day. Dr. Jim Loehr, a famous performance psychologist, is one of the originators of pioneering mental toughness. Recently the term has acquired a broader use in business, sports and coaches. These days it is used by business professionals, performers and athletes to achieve groundbreaking results. For athletes it has helped them to become better and cope with the challenges of training and competition.

A number of studies have directly linked mental toughness to sporting success and achievements. There are several reasons that contribute to mental toughness influencing success. In the case of sports, athletes need to be able to believe in themselves whilst handling pressure and avoiding negative distractions. Their desire to win must be so strong that it overcomes any other smaller desires. Mental toughness is what will set them apart from the other athletes. The same can be said in business and life. If you have the mental toughness to believe in yourself, avoid distractions and handle pressure then you are likely to achieve great success.

With a natural or trained psychological edge of mental toughness it will enable you to much more effectively deal with the challenges and demands of pursuing your goals. That could be in the office, gym or at home. Under times of pressure it will help you become more consistent, focused, confident and controlled. The skill of mental toughness is a valuable asset in all areas of life. Those who train it increase their chances of rising to higher levels of success and excelling in life.

Incidentally mental toughness should be learned and developed by anyone who wishes to improve themselves and produce higher level results. Whether that is in work, sports or life. It can all be applied. Business people, sales teams and entrepreneurs will benefit in big ways from it because they are typically working in high pressure environments. Mental toughness would help them to overcome challenges, believe they can do it and stay focused on achieving their goals. In sports of course mental toughness is a key component towards success.

Lastly, it could help in many areas of your personal life. Maybe you're in a difficult relationship and you need to keep believing in it and have the courage to take the first step towards fixing it. Mental toughness again will help you here. For parents it's great too. Children of any age can put a huge level of stress on parents. It will help you to deal with the challenges, pressures and stress of being a parent.

Can mental toughness be learned?

Yes, there are a number of ways to learn mental toughness. To begin, start reading more about it. A great primer would be the books and research by Dr Jim Loehr. "Mentally Tough" and "Toughness Training For Life" are both great primers on the subject.

Just like a muscle, mental toughness needs to be exercised so that it can grow. This needs to be done consistently and you need to push your limits. Showing up at the gym once a week won't get you decent results. Neither will you get results if you stick with the same weights. Pushing yourself through the difficulty is when you grow and gain stronger mental toughness. For example you set out to do nine reps on the weights bench. Push for that one more rep! Or you're working on a business task. You're getting tired and want to eat a snack. Push for thirty minutes more of work.

Expanding your comfort zone and going beyond what you thought was possible will make you stronger. Working with others who are achieving at a higher level than you is also great for this. Often when we are alone we let the pressure off and don't really reach our limits. Having a high achiever around you will help you to break some of your own limits. If you can't find that person then read biographies of people who overcame huge obstacles to achieve amazing things. I recommend the biography of the greatest boxer of all time, Muhammid Ali. He refused to serve in the war against Vietnam because he didn't believe in it. The U.S government stripped him of his titles for four years and banned him from boxing. Against all odds, he came back four years later and won his titles back.

There will be days when you don't feel like doing anything. Motivation comes and goes. But when it's not there is when your mental toughness kicks in. Build consistent empowering habits and the tough times will become easier because it is a pattern of behaviour. The easy way is the hard way. Be consistent and develop a positive mindset. This is the first thing you need to do to increase mental toughness. As we now know the mind is filled with thoughts and most of those are repeated or negative. It's like a huge weight on your back, pulling you down. Trying to achieve something with that extra weight on you is only going to make things more difficult. Why not dump that extra weight and save your strength for the most useful challenges?

Let go of any self limiting beliefs

Those are just holding you back. If we allow these self limiting beliefs to control our minds that it overwhelms our ability to think positively. Become aware of your self-limiting beliefs. Take note of them. Question if they are helping you. Question if they are true. Reframe them in a positive way. Affirm those new beliefs.

Break free from all or nothing thinking

This is another form of negative thinking that is crowding your mind with useless negativity. Recognize this as when you're thinking in extremes. For example, you are either great or you are a loser. You either did well or you suck. It's very black and white thinking that is not helping you.

In the real world it can play out like this. Say you wanted to earn $5000 in a month but you earned $4700. In that case then you're not a loser. Because you gained, you did well! Or you wanted to bench press 120kg but you hit 115kg. Still a great effort. Shoot for the stars and reach the moon. Don't allow this all or nothing thinning to corrupt your mind. Be grateful for

Overthinking

the in betweens. All those other shades of success. Focus on the positive. Be constructive in your self criticism and make sure it is acknowledging your success and being constructive towards improvement.

Stop dwelling on the negative. When you dwell on negatives it is wasting more mental energy that could be used in a positive direction. If you want to become mentally tougher then you have to ditch the dwelling. Move on from your failures. Learn from them. Think higher about the future. Expect good things. When things don't work out for you or you face a challenge, sure you can allow yourself to feel disappointment or frustration. That is a normal reaction. Just try to reduce the amount of time that you spend dwelling on it. Be constructive. Seek advice from other people to get a new perspective. Set yourself a time limit to think constructively about it. Journal about it and get it out there on paper. Calm yourself down and examine it with a clear mind. The quicker you can get over this and achieve a solution the quicker you can move towards achieving the success you want in your life.

Connect with your life purpose

A critical element of mental toughness is to have a strong and focused mind. When you have a strong reason or rather a strong life purpose then it will keep you from getting distracted, discouraged or side tracked from your mission. When that setback comes you figure out a way forward. Usually when we get thrown off we give up. That's not about willpower or discipline. It's just about having strong enough reasons to keep going.

When the going gets tough the tough get going. When things get tough people usually will escape to work on something easier. But for mentally tough people they will dig in and try to keep going. This is life. It will throw challenges at you. Those will require courage, resilience and mental toughness. Most of that comes down to being a consistent person. If you keep showing up it gets easier because you get stronger. Learn to have a hard working ethic. Put in the effort daily and become consistent with it. You will be able to deal with those challenges easier when they come up. It rains or you feel tired. No worries, you're already up and ready to go because you were made for this. It's a habit.

"It's not about how hard you hit. It's about how hard you can get hit and keep moving forward. How much you can take and keep moving forward." — Rocky balboa / Sylvester Stallone

No matter who you are, achieving success can be difficult. It will require your physical, mental and emotional energy. You will be faced with ups and downs, failures, burnouts, limiting beliefs, discouragement and much more. With so much stacked against you it can be easy to just quit. Mental toughness is the key to succeeding. It isn't about talent or having passion. It's your ability to stick with something when things become tough. Those who can push beyond obstacles will achieve their dreams. No matter who you are, you can become more mentally tough. No matter who you are, you can push through and achieve your dreams.

"It never gets easier you just get better.", Jordan Hoechlin

Thomas Swain

Conclusion

Here we are at the conclusion of this book about overthinking. I hope that you've discovered some new insights and solutions to dealing with your overthinking. Now that we are here, let's take a moment to summarise the main points and promises.

To begin with we discovered that the human brain has limitless potential and can be much more powerful than even the latest supercomputers. However, we also discovered that we are still falling victim to our primal instincts which haven't evolved since we were being hunted by predators. Clearly those are outdated. The world we now live in is a much safer place. Yet it is such an energetic and abundant place that can be overwhelming. Which causes us to overthink.

With our understanding of our biology and the world around us, my promise then was to explore the root causes of overthinking. Exploring the causes of overthinking was our first step to take towards freedom. Identifying the source is an effective way to get to the root of the problem and to then seek solutions. Beginning with the first cause, stress. For many of us stress is a distinct part of everyday life. Many common causes of stress are affecting us. From stress at work to finances to family to health and to life in general. Stress can affect our behaviour, mood, mental and even physical symptoms. With a better understanding of stress we then explored how to deal with stress.

In brief you should review your lifestyle and build healthy habits. Some of those might include exercise, going to bed at a good time and cutting out any vices or bad influences. If stress from your lifestyle or work is causing your overthinking then be honest with yourself about the source of it. Reach out for help from friends and colleagues if necessary. They could help you to identify new solutions and perspectives which will help you to take clear steps forward.

The next cause we explored was anxiety. We discovered that anxiety is a normal emotion and many people feel it on a mild level but it becomes an issue when we're faced with stronger anxiety disorders. Managing anxiety is about getting to the root of the problem and exploring what causes it. Once we've dealt with what the causes are, we can focus on solutions. Those include maintaining good health, focusing on the right things and having an effective system of relaxation.

Following on we explored depression and rumination which affects nearly ten percent of the adult US population. In fact many people from all over the world suffer from the effects of it. Overthinkers are often left feeling depressed which further submerges into a negative cycle of lowering thoughts. Sleep, eating, concentration and much more are affected by this. Unfortunately we discovered that there isn't a magic pill or quick fix solution to depression. However we can learn to effectively deal with it by pushing back on it, challenging our thoughts and having more positive influences in our life. Take action, make plans of things to do with your time and stay connected with your friends and family.

Exploring one more cause of overthinking we explored information overload in our world. In this current age, information is coming at us at hyperspeed. Trying to focus or make decisions in such a hectic world has become challenging. Basically it causes us to overthink. Dealing with such a huge challenge begins with eliminating the non-essential and doing more of what you love. Take accountability for how you spend your time and make sure that you're doing the things that you want to do with the people who you want to be with. In addition, become a more organised person. To be effective you need to remove distractions. Minimalism is a great concept for being more effective and organized. In that chapter we discovered how having less will reduce your mental storage. Then you can focus on what matters. Which in turn leads us to making better decisions. In addition we identified some other ways to make better decisions. In brief those included; setting time limits, using decision models and taking the time out to think.

Next we looked at managing insomnia naturally without sleeping pills. A common issue for overthinkers is sleep. Not enough, too much or inconsistency. Let it be more natural. Have a consistent sleep schedule. Take enough time to relax before sleep. Finally we explored medical conditions briefly. Again let me state that if you suffer from any medical issues then you should seek medical professional advice.

In the next chapter we explored negative thoughts and negativity bias. Evidently some people suffer more than others with negativity. In fact most people have a leaning towards being more negative. This is known as the negativity bias. In summary humans are prone to leaning towards negative thoughts as an automatic reaction. In this chapter we explored the causes of those negative thoughts. Indeed negative thoughts can feel incredibly real. We can get lost in them and they can take over our minds. As I mentioned, first of all you need to become aware of your obsessive thoughts. Notice the ones that are not productive and challenge them. It is then that you can work on replacing them with more rational thoughts. With work it will soon become a habit and an evolution of your thinking as it becomes much more healthy. Instead of obsessing over negative thoughts the aim will be to develop a new mindset. Instead of being a victim of your thoughts, think what you can do about it.

Take that seriously because that directly affects your health and your immune system. Start to rewire and deal with negative thoughts so that they don't destroy your life.

We explored some simple ways to deal with negative thoughts. Firstly we looked at acceptance and commitment therapy (ACT). In summary this is a method of reconfiguring your relationship to your thoughts. Overthinking is diffused by exploring the thoughts to gain more control on them. Essentially it's reframing those thoughts to be more positive. In addition we looked at some more ways to deal with negative thoughts. Those included challenging your thoughts, focusing on your feelings, socialising, maintaining great health, having fun and distraction. We also looked at journalling and cognitive restructuring which can help to modify your thoughts so that you become better at managing the conditions and causes of overthinking. All of these as direct results can give you increased optimism to help you to deal with addictions and in turn more confidence. In that chapter you can find the steps to cognitive restructuring to gain the benefits immediately.

Moving forwards we took it up a notch and explored positivity. Now this is something that's thrown around a lot these days but for a good reason. We also explored the states of optimism and pessimism and how they can again impact on your health and overthinking. Naturally we concluded that positive thinking is a much better way of thinking. That begins with positive and correct self talk. We have to realise that the mind is always going to keep producing thoughts and we need to take responsibility to make sure that those are the right thoughts. Positive ones are much better. In that chapter we explored curating positive influences so that you're constantly filling and receiving positive influences in your life instead of being a victim of the negativity in the world. Truth is that there's so much to be grateful for. Change the channel and tune into positive inputs.

Additionally in this chapter we explored self-esteem and how it plays a key role in mental wellness and overthinking. We explored how to improve your self-esteem and how to work on improving any negative self-esteem issues. In that chapter you will find specific ways to improve your self-esteem, grow your strengths to become your own best friend. In addition you can find some useful information about the hierarchy of needs which plays a crucial role in self-esteem.

Moving on we explored more techniques, tactics and mindsets, beginning with meditation and mindfulness. Many of the concepts in this book stem from the concepts of mediation and mindfulness. Both have been proven again and again to improve brain focus and function. They are an excellent remedy to overthinking and in turn a better quality of life in general. We explored how to implement mindfulness along with meditation into your daily life. Then you can enjoy the benefits right away. These are simple but highly effective skills and concepts that few people really master or utilize. With daily practice they can effectively cure your overthinking. Live in the present moment and it will become easier to break free from what happened in the past or what might happen in the future.

In the next chapter we looked at more techniques, tactics and mindsets to improve your brain function and to deal with overthinking more effectively. First we looked at self awareness as a way to be more in the present moment. Great stuff. Again we looked at challenging your own thinking with questions. Then we looked at thinking big which is an excellent way to make your thoughts much more personal purposeful. Furthermore we took a look at how distraction, philosophical razors and changing your stories can all lead to a more effective way of thinking. Finally we looked at how exercise, journalling, setting goals and so on will lead you to a more purposeful way of life. In effect these reduce your overthinking since there's more purpose and more doing what you love.

Additionally at the end of that chapter we explored mental toughness which is a tool used by professional athletes and business people. It is something that sets those successful people apart from the rest and contributes to influencing their success. In fact this can be used by anyone to produce higher results in work, sports and life. We concluded that it can be learnt by anyone and in that chapter you can find out just how mental toughness can be applied to you. Overcome the challenges and deal with overthinking to help you focus on what matters. This will help you connect with your life purpose and stop overthinking.

Achieving success can be difficult. You'll be faced with ups and downs. Overthinking can be a major obstacle. But through the knowledge in this book you can rise above it. Declutter your mind and take responsibility for what you put into it. Stay healthy and practice positive habits. When the going gets tough the tough get going.

Revisit this book or a particular chapter again and again. You may see things from a new perspective. You may gain new insights. Or you may find a solution to a problem you're facing right now. The one thing that I would like you to take away from this book is that you are in control of your destiny. No longer do you need to be a victim of overthinking. What was presented in this book was an effective diagnosis and solutions. It is a new way of life.

Now take hold of the reins of your new new life and venture out into the world a better you.

> **Start Your Week The Right Way**
>
> We've all had that sinking feeling on a Sunday night, when you remember it's Monday tomorrow and the weekend is over. It can be tricky trying to launch ourselves back into work-mode, but with the right motivation and mentality, you can get your week off to the perfect start.
>
> Receive evidence-based guidance, up-to-date resources, and first-hand accounts to help you.

Sign Up Now & You will receive this newsletter every Monday.

https://www.subscribepage.com/tswain

References

12 Rules for Life: An Antidote to Chaos. (2018). Allen Lane.

Ackerman, C. E. (2020, December 14). How Does Acceptance And Commitment Therapy (ACT) Work? PositivePsychology.Com. https://positivepsychology.com/act-acceptance-and-commitment-therapy/

Ali, M. (1978). Ali: Born Again! Newsweek, 4–10.

American Psychological Association, A. P. A. (n.d.). Anxiety. https://Www.Apa.Org/ https://www.apa.org/topics/anxiety

Cameron, K., & Caza, A. (2008). Positive Organizational Scholarship: What Does it Achieve? SSRN Electronic Journal. Published. https://doi.org/10.2139/ssrn.1295299

Dar, K. A., & Iqbal, N. (2014). Worry and Rumination in Generalized Anxiety Disorder and Obsessive Compulsive Disorder. The Journal of Psychology, 149(8), 866–880. https://doi.org/10.1080/00223980.2014.986430

Depression: Facts, Statistics, and You. (2018). Health Line. https://www.healthline.com/health/depression/facts-statistics-infographic

Ellis, A., Harper, R. A., & Powers, M. (1975). A Guide to Rational Living (3rd ed.). Wilshire Book Company. Cognitive Restructuring

Ferriss, T., & Schwarzenegger, A. (2016). TOOLS OF TITANS. Penguin Random House UK.

Frankl, V. E. (2004). Man's Search for Meaning (New Ed). Ebury Pr.

Harvard Health. (2011, October 11). Writing about emotions may ease stress and trauma. https://www.health.harvard.edu/healthbeat/writing-about-emotions-may-ease-stress-and-trauma

Hölzel, B. K., Carmody, J., Vangel, M., Congleton, C., Yerramsetti, S. M., Gard, T., & Lazar, S. W. (2011). Mindfulness practice leads to increases in regional brain gray matter density. Psychiatry Research: Neuroimaging, 191(1), 36–43.
https://doi.org/10.1016/j.pscychresns.2010.08.006

Jordan, H. (2020). [interview quote circa 2020]. Interview with Jordan Hoechlin.

Kabat-Zinn, J. (2005). Wherever You Go, There You Are: Mindfulness Meditation in Everyday Life (10th ed.). Hachette Books.

Lazar, S. W., Kerr, C. E., Wasserman, R. H., Gray, J. R., Greve, D. N., Treadway, M. T., McGarvey, M., Quinn, B. T., Dusek, J. A., Benson, H., Rauch, S. L., Moore, C. I., & Fischl, B. (2005). Meditation experience is associated with increased cortical thickness. NeuroReport, 16(17), 1893–1897.
https://doi.org/10.1097/01.wnr.0000186598.66243.19

Lee, B. (1973). [interview quote circa 1973]. Interview with Bruce Lee

Loehr, J. E. (1994). Toughness Training for Life: A Revolutionary Program for Maximizing Health, Happiness and Productivity. Plume.

Maslow, A. H. (2011). Hierarchy of Needs: A Theory of Human Motivation. www.all-about-psychology.com.

NBC. (2010). Arianna Huffington interview quote. http://inc.com/ & NBC. https://www.nbcnews.com/id/wbna35018305

NIMH » 5 Things You Should Know About Stress. (2021, May 31). NIMH. https://www.nimh.nih.gov/health/publications/stress/

Ockham, W. O., Adams, M. M., & Kretzmann, N. (1983). Predestination, God's Foreknowledge, And Future Contingents (Hackett Classics) (2nd ed.). Hackett Publishing Company, Inc.

Robbins, T. (1992). Awaken the Giant Within : How to Take Immediate Control of Your Mental, Emotional, Physical and Financial Destiny! Simon & Schuster.

Schwartz, B. (2016). The Paradox of Choice: Why More Is Less, Revised Edition (Revised ed.). Ecco.

Schwartz, D. J. (1987). The Magic of Thinking Big (Reprint ed.). Fireside.

Seligman, M. E. P. (2006). Learned Optimism: How to Change Your Mind and Your Life (Reprint ed.). Vintage.

Seneca, L. A., & Campbell, R. (1969). Letters from a Stoic (Penguin Classics) (Reprint ed.). Penguin Books.

Sylvester, S. (Director). (1979). Rocky Balboa [Film]. Sony Pictures Releasing

Szegedy-Maszak, M. (2005). Mysteries of the mind. http://webhome.auburn.edu/~mitrege/ENGL2210/USNWR-mind.html

V., Raymond, E. S., & Steele, G. L. (2011). The Jargon File, Version 2.9.10, 01 Jul 1992. Caiman.

Virgin Records. (1979). Always Look on the Bright Side of Life. Eric Idle (Monty Python)

www.ingramcontent.com/pod-product-compliance
Lightning Source LLC
Chambersburg PA
CBHW070106120526
44588CB00032B/1248